THE

ULTIMATE

HOLLYWOOD

TOUR BOOK

The Ultimate

The Incomparable Guide to Movie Stars' Homes, Suicides, and All the

TOUR BOOK

Movie and TV Locations, Scandals, Murders, Famous Tourist Sites

By
William A. Gordon

NORTH RIDGE BOOKS

OTHER BOOKS BY WILLIAM A. GORDON

THE FOURTH OF MAY
Killings and Coverups at Kent State

"HOW MANY BOOKS DO YOU SELL IN OHIO?"
A Quote Book for Writers

In Memory of
Professor Dennis Gordon
1915—1989

North Ridge Books Permissions Department
P.O. Box 2314
Toluca Lake, CA 91610

Fifth Printing 1994

10 9 8 7 6 5

Library of Congress Cataloging-in-Publication Data
  Gordon, William A.
  The ultimate Hollywood tour book: the incomparable guide to
  movie stars' homes, movie and TV locations, scandals, murders,
  suicides, and all the famous tourist sites / William A.
  Gordon--First Ed.
  p. cm.
  ISBN 0-937813-03-6
  1. Motion picture actors and actresses--Homes and haunts--
California--Los Angeles—Guidebooks. 2. Motion Picture locations-
California--Los Angeles--Guidebooks. 3. Hollywood (Los Angeles,
Calif.)--Guidebooks. 4. Motion picture actors and actresses--
Biography--Miscellanea. 5. Hollywood (Los Angeles, Calif.)--Social
life and customs.
  I. Title
PN1993.5.U65G635 1992
791.43'09794'940904 9--dc20

ISBN 0-937813-03-6
LC 92-060227

CONTENTS

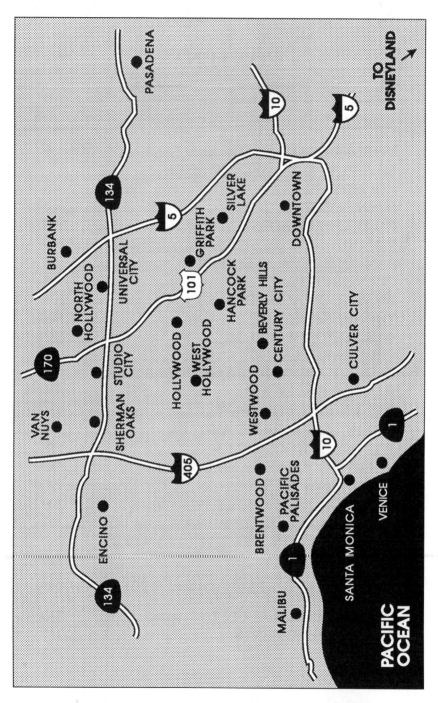

MAP 1   GREATER LOS ANGELES

☆ INTRODUCTION

The Ultimate Hollywood Tour Book was written for the millions of people who visit Southern California each year, and who, not knowing how to find the real attractions of Tinseltown, take prepackaged bus tours to celebrities' homes or who go on studio tours which show you only what the studios want you to see.

This book will take you to places you will not be shown on any organized tour. We will show you where the major stars of both today and yesteryear live. Stars such as Madonna, Elvis Presley, Marilyn Monroe, Arnold Schwarzenegger, Cher, and Tom Cruise.

The Ultimate Hollywood Tour Book will show you where you have the best chances of actually seeing the stars. Although it is always fun to see where they live, you probably will not see them outside their gated mansions and homes. However, there is a good chance you will see someone famous if you go to one of the dozens of restaurants, hotels, or hot spots that attract a celebrity clientele. Dozens of such establishments are profiled in this book.

We will show you where, throughout greater Los Angeles, dozens of classic or highly popular motion pictures have been filmed. Movies such as *E.T., The Terminator, Terminator II, Bugsy, Planet of the Apes,* the *Back to the Future* series, *Beverly Hills Cop I* and *II, The Player, Chinatown,* and *Father of the Bride.*

We will show you how to find famous locations

such as the "L.A. Law Building," "The Bat Cave," and the houses seen in popular television shows: "Dynasty," "The Brady . Bunch," "Thirtysomething," "Doogie Howser, M.D.," and "Beverly Hills 90210."

We will show you where some of Hollywood's most notorious murders, suicides, and scandals have occurred. You will see where the Manson clan struck (in a home Candice Bergen lived in just a few months earlier), where Marilyn Monroe committed suicide, where John Belushi and Janet Joplin overdosed, and the Menendez brothers allegedly gunned down their own parents in cold blood.

We will take you to other locations that may surprise you. How many of you know, for example, that John Dean, the man who brought down Richard Nixon's presidency, now lives in Beverly Hills? Or that Nixon himself lived in Brentwood after losing the 1960 election? Would you like to see where John F. Kennedy's most notorious mistress lived? Or where Ronald Reagan lived when he was elected president—or where he lives now? Virtually all of Reagan's Hollywood residences can be found in this book.

We will also show you how to find the major studios and world-famous attractions such as Mann's Chinese Theater and the popular Universal Studios Tour.

The focus of this book, of course, is not on the commercial attractions or the usual tourist traps. The tours and the television ticket outlets are included because you cannot write a guide book about Hollywood and not mention them.

The emphasis in this book is on the hidden or unpublicized attractions—the ones that Hollywood insiders know about, but which tourists usually never know exist.

10

An important point needs to be made at the outset. When I refer to Hollywood, both in the title and throughout the book, I refer not just to the geographical community within the city of Los Angeles where most of early motion picture history was made. I refer to Hollywood, the entertainment industry, which today is spread out throughout all of Southern California.

Ironically, many tourists find Hollywood, the community, to be the most disappointing part of their trips. Many tourists come to Hollywood looking for movie stars, glamorous settings, and palm trees. What they often find instead are panhandlers, teen-agers who look like they have taken too many drugs, and tacky souvenir shops lining Hollywood Boulevard.

I certainly do not want to suggest that little of note happens in Hollywood the community today, that Hollywood is not trying to revitalize itself, or that the community is not worth seeing. In fact, I cannot imagine anyone touring Southern California and not seeing Hollywood the community.

The point here is simply that this book focuses on the present. And while I have tried to pay homage to Hollywood's past (particularly its glamour days in the 1920s, 1930s, and 1940s), this is primarily a book on how Hollywood of the 1990s lives, works, and plays.

This book is arranged geographically, and starts with a self-guided tour of the celebrity homes in the so-called Platinum Triangle: Beverly Hills, Bel-Air and the lesser known, but actually more expensive residential area, Holmby Hills.

Maps to these celebrity homes are hawked on seemingly every street corner along Sunset Boulevard and in every souvenir shop in town. The tour presented in this book is very different than what those maps offer. For one, the maps in this book are up to date (and are updated in each edition). More importantly, the addresses have been verified through searches of public records showing who owns what property.

The Ultimate Hollywood Tour Book is also the first Hollywood tour book to show not only where the major celebrities of the past and present live (or have lived), but also to tell something about the history of these homes.

(Incidentally, the people who sell the maps to the stars' homes on the street corners would have you believe that most motion picture and television stars live in Beverly Hills or Bel-Air. Actually, only about 25% of the best-known living actors live on the streets covered in the "Maps to the Stars' Homes." As this book shows, celebrities live all over greater Los Angeles. Observant readers will also note that the younger stars tend to live in the Hollywood Hills and in the outlying areas. Hardly any celebrity under the age of 40 lives in Beverly Hills.)

Subsequent chapters highlight celebrity homes, movie locations, historic entertainment industry sites, and other points of interest in Brentwood, Pacific Palisades, Malibu, Venice and Santa Monica, Culver City, Westwood and Century City, the Sunset Strip and West Hollywood, Fairfax and the Miracle Mile, Hancock Park and the Wilshire District, downtown Los Angeles, the Hollywood Hills, Pasadena, the San Fernando Valley, and, of course, Hollywood itself.

Although the tours presented here very roughly circle the city, the author realizes that tourists will start from many different points of town and will, instead of following any sequence presented, tour the areas that are either closest to them or are of most interest to them.

To make the most of your trip to Los Angeles, I suggest reading this book first, choosing the areas of greatest interest, and using the maps provided, combining the tours as you see fit. (For example, tours of the Sunset Strip and Beverly Hills can be very easily combined.)

There is really a great deal to see—and you will find, despite rumors to the contrary, that Los Angeles is one of the greatest places in the world to go sightseeing. In fact, that is why I live here: because I get to go sightseeing every day.

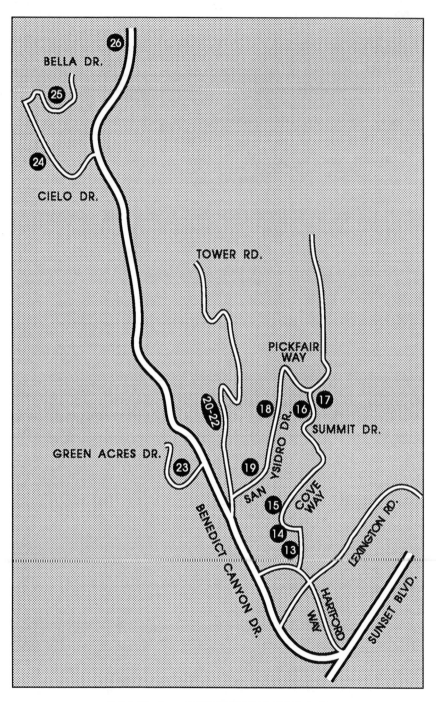

MAP 3 BEVERLY HILLS

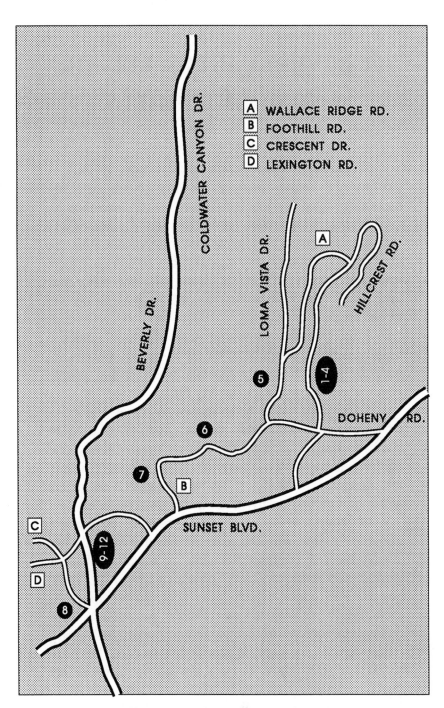

MAP 2   BEVERLY HILLS

☆ BEVERLY HILLS, BEL-AIR AND HOLMBY HILLS

Whenever I show people around Beverly Hills, I like to get behind one of the tour buses, tell my passengers what the tour guides are saying, and then let my passengers know who really lives in these homes.

I do not mean to suggest that most of the tours are unreliable, or in any way disreputable (although I have heard one person indirectly affiliated with one major tour joke about "the new lies our guides are making up this week").

I am merely suggesting that the tour guides— usually aspiring actors between gigs—have, on occasion, used their highly creative talents when telling people about who lives where in Beverly Hills.

Tour guides have been known to move celebrities from one street to another—or from one part of town to another—just to spice up the tours. One might say that they sometimes play a version of celebrity musical chairs just to have something to say while driving on streets where no one particularly notable has lived on.

Of course, there is another, probably even more important reason why the tours of Beverly Hills do not always meet the highest standards of accuracy. That is because the tours are based on the maps to the stars' homes. The maps—which have been around since at least 1924 (real estate agents used to publish them themselves to lure prospective home buyers to Beverly Hills)—are an inescapable part of life in L.A. They are hawked on seemingly every street corner along Sunset

Boulevard in Beverly Hills and in virtually every souvenir shop along Hollywood Boulevard. You can even find the maps in vending machines at the public information center of the Los Angeles Convention and Visitors Bureau.

The best-selling map is called simply "Map of Movie Stars' Homes." Even though celebrities move as often, if not more often, than regular folk, the current edition is remarkably similar to a 1977 edition of the same map on file at the Beverly Hills Public Library.

The reason the mapmakers do not keep up with celebrity comings and goings is because they have no incentive to. After all, their customers never know the difference. Tourists who are in town for a short period do not have the time or the inclination to independently verify the information they are given—even if they knew how to.

Of course, there are a few people in Hollywood who like to keep up with the latest celebrity real estate transactions.

You are lucky. I happen to be one of them.

The following tour, which tourists can follow in lieu of paying $20 to $30 to go on a bus tour, brings Beverly Hills touring into the 1990s and reflects who lives, or has lived, in the houses in Beverly Hills, Bel-Air and Holmby Hills, each time we go back to press (which is at least once and often twice a year).

I have included driving directions to help the reader get around Beverly Hills, but I have not done so for most other parts of town. Beverly Hills is a special case. Its residential streets twist and turn so much that they often look like pretzels. Not only are the streets sometimes confusing for the uninitiated, but several of the streets change names in midcourse—and sometimes more than once. A recent story in the *Los Angeles Times* told the story of typical tourists who found following the existing maps to stars' homes so frustrating that they gave up and went to the beach instead. The directions which accompany the text and maps should make your sightseeing a more enjoyable experience.

Please note: These houses are private residences. You can drive by them, admire them, and be what we call a "lookie-loo;" but you should never, ever disturb the privacy of these individuals.

If you approach a celebrity at his or her home, he or she may construe the approach as a hostile act and act accordingly.

Remember: not all celebrities are as volatile as Sean Penn or Sean Young. But why take a chance?

Also: while it is always possible you may see celebrities outside their houses (I've seen Madonna jogging, Ted Danson's kids playing, and Valerie Harper walking her dogs), any such sightings are strictly up to chance. The likelihood is that you will not see celebrities outside their homes.

If you want to see movie stars, go to one of the many restaurants or hotels they frequent. This book lists dozens of establishments where you have a good chance of seeing someone famous.

The following tour should be taken just to get a general sense of how and where celebrities and Los Angeles' upper class live.

(DIRECTIONS: This tour starts at the intersection of Sunset Boulevard and Hillcrest Drive, which is located one mile east of Beverly Hills Hotel and just west of the Sunset Strip. You will be traveling north on Hillcrest Drive. If are you on Sunset headed east, make a left turn onto Hillcrest Drive. If you are coming from Hollywood or the Sunset Strip and headed west, turn right.)

1-4. CELEBRITY HOUSES ON HILLCREST DRIVE

On this street, north of Sunset, you can see the home of Morey Amsterdam, who played Buddy on "The Dick Van Dyke Show" (1012 Hillcrest Drive), and the long-time home of comedian Groucho Marx (1083 Hillcrest Drive).

If you continue north past Wallace Ridge, you can also see, at 1174 Hillcrest, the split-level French-regency style house that Elvis bought in May 1967 shortly after his marriage to Priscilla. Elvis did not live in that house for very long. A few months after buying this house, he decided he wanted to buy a home that afforded more privacy, and moved to 144 Monovale Drive, the last of several homes in which he lived in Los Angeles. That last home, which is featured later in this tour, is probably the more interesting of the two.

Comedian Danny Thomas lived in a mansion he called Villa Roisa at 1187 Hillcrest Drive, which is at the end of the street; and it was there, on May 21, 1980, that his daughter, Marlo, married talk show host Phil Donahue. The best place to view the Thomas estate, though, is not from up close, but from a distance on Wallace Ridge.

In Beverly Hills, even the mailboxes are special.

Instead of continuing on Hillcrest, make a left turn onto Wallace Ridge and stop around 1120 Wallace Ridge, a pink mansion that the rock star Prince once lived in and which tour guides still point out as his. If you look to your left can see Thomas' home from across the ravine. It is the last home on the right of the mountain.

After viewing Thomas' estate, continue down Wallace Ridge and make a left onto Loma Vista Drive.

5. GREYSTONE MANSION, 905 Loma Vista Drive

This magnificent 55-room mansion, built in 1923, was the largest and most expensive home in Beverly Hills in the 1920s. It was built by oilman Edward Doheny—the same Edward Doheny who was embroiled in the Teapot Dome scandal. Doheny, who was not content with his personal fortune of $100,000,000, was accused of paying President Warren G. Harding's Secretary of the Interior, Albert Fall, a $100,000 bribe in return for secret leases to government oil reserves at Elk Hills and Buena Vista in California. His trial ended in an acquittal. In 1928 Doheny built the mansion as a gift for his only son, Edward Jr., who moved in with his wife and children. A few weeks later, however, Edward Jr. and his male secretary, Hugh Plunkett, were both found dead in Doheny's bedroom, giving rise to unconfirmed rumors that they died in a lovers' quarrel.

Edward Jr.'s widow continued to live at Greystone until 1955, when Henry Crown, the owner of the Empire State Building, paid $25 million for the estate and subdivided it. What remained of the property was subsequently leased to the American Film Institute, and is now a public park owned and operated by the city of Beverly Hills.

If you stop at Greystone, do not be surprised to see movie crews. The mansion and grounds have frequently been used as a movie location, and the films *Ghostbusters* (where it was used as Gracie Mansion), *All of Me, The Witches of Eastwick, Guilty by Suspicion, The Fabulous Baker Boys, The Marrying Man, Memoirs of an Invisible Man, Death Becomes Her, The Bodyguard,* as well as the television programs such as "Dynasty," "Falcon Crest," and "Knots Landing" have all been filmed here.

(DIRECTIONS: After leaving Greystone, make a right turn onto Loma Vista Drive and then another right onto Doheny Drive.)

6. MERV GRIFFIN'S HOME, 603 N. Doheny Drive (northwest corner of Schuyler Road)

(DIRECTIONS: After seeing Merv's place, continue on Doheny Drive, then make a left turn onto Foothill Road.)

7. HOME OWNED BY FRANK SINATRA, 915 Foothill Road

Frank Sinatra owns the mansion at 915 Foothill Road, and MCA Chairperson Lew Wasserman lives next door at 911 Foothill Road. (MCA is the parent company of Universal Studios.)

(DIRECTIONS: Make a right at Sunset Boulevard, and continue going west three blocks until you see the sign that reads: "Beverly Drive/Crescent Drive." The Beverly Hills Hotel is just past Crescent Drive.)

8. BEVERLY HILLS HOTEL AND BUNGALOWS, 9641 Sunset Boulevard, (310) 276-2251; (800) 283-8885

The Beverly Hills Hotel is one of the most famous hotels in the world. It was built by developer Burton Green in 1912, and it is often said that almost every one of the richest, most powerful, or most famous people on Earth has stayed here at one time or another. Some members of Britain's royal family consider it a home away from home. Famous American guests include the extraordinarily eccentric billionaire, Howard Hughes, who stayed at the hotel off and on for almost thirty years, even though he owned several houses in Los Angeles during that time. According to the hotel's press kits, Hughes was known to order roast beef sandwiches and then require the hotel staff to hide them in trees for him. Hughes had one of his nervous breakdowns in Bungalow 4. Bungalow 5 is favored by former *TV Guide* publisher Walter Annenberg, who stays at the hotel for

The Beverly Hills Hotel.

five to six weeks every summer. Marilyn Monroe reportedly had affairs with John and Robert Kennedy in other bungalows, and Elizabeth Taylor shared bungalows there with six of her first seven husbands (Nicky Hilton, who owned his own hotels, was reportedly the lone exception).

The hotel's celebrated Polo Lounge has been described by the *Los Angeles Times* "as much a stage and an office where entertainment industry executives make deals as it is a restaurant . . . [It is] the best improvisational theater in town."

The hotel is owned by the Sultan of Brunei. The Sultan paid $185 million for the hotel in 1987, $50 million more than previous owner, Marvin Davis, paid.

Rates for one-bedrooms start at $170 a night.

(Note: The hotel will be closed for renovations in late 1992 and 1993.)

9-12. CELEBRITY HOMES ON BEVERLY DRIVE

On each of the streets surrounding the Beverly Hills Hotel you can see some of the most impressive estates in Beverly Hills. In fact, it almost does not matter which direction you proceed from here. There is something worth seeing in virtually every direction.

When you approach the hotel from Sunset Boulevard, the sign that reads "Beverly Drive/Crescent Drive" will alert you to the fact that there are actually two streets on the east side of the hotel. Some of the organized tours, as they approach the hotel from Sunset Boulevard, make an immediate right at Beverly Drive; others make a far right turn at Crescent Drive, where Gloria Swanson and Milton Berle lived at 904 and 908 N. Crescent Drive, respectively. If Swanson's and Berle's former homes interest you, make a right turn from Sunset onto Crescent, and then a left at the first street, Lexington Drive. You will wind up at the exact same location as if you had made a right turn onto Beverly Drive.

From Sunset Boulevard, make a right turn onto Beverly Drive, a street that was once owned in its entirety by Beverly Hills' first mayor, humorist and silent film star, Will Rogers. Rogers had a home at 925 N. Beverly until about 1928, when he moved to Pacific Palisades (p. 74). Pat Boone still lives at 904 Beverly Drive. Carolyn Jones, who played Morticia in the television series "The Addams Family," lived at 907 Beverly, and "M*A*S*H." star Wayne Rogers still lives at 916 Beverly.

If you continue north on Beverly Drive, Beverly will turn into Coldwater Canyon Drive, one of the major thoroughfares connecting Beverly Hills with the San Fernando Valley.

It is possible to take a side trip north on Coldwater Canyon; however, from Beverly, the author recommends taking a left turn onto Lexington Road. Continue half a mile to Hartford Way, make a right on Hartford Way, and then an immediate right to Cove Way, which will lead you to the homes of Sidney Poitier and then the one-time homes of David O. Selznick, Charlie Chaplin, Douglas Fairbanks, Jr. and Mary Pickford, and Sammy Davis, Jr.

13. HOME OF SIDNEY POITIER, 1007 Cove Way

Poitier was the first black actor to win an Oscar (for his performance in *Lillies of the Field*.) He was also one of Hollywood's first black directors.

CELEBRITIES WHO LIVE ON COLDWATER CANYON: Chuck Woolery, Deborah Shelton, Mel Torme, Barry Diller, Jeanne Cooper, and Charlton Heston. A number of celebrities also live on the various side streets off Coldwater Canyon: Marilyn Beck, Corbin Bernsen, Tom Bosley, Joan Collins, Sid Caesar, Brandon Tartikoff, Faye Dunaway, Barbara Eden, John Fogerty, George Peppard, Esther Williams, Clive Barker, Bette Midler, Theresa Russell, Christine McVie, James Woods, Woody Harrelson, Michael Cimino, Don Johnson and Melanie Griffith, Vanna White, Jane Seymour, Susan Dey, Connie Stevens, Gabe Kaplan, Angie Dickinson, and Jami Gertz.

John Landis has directed many comedies, including *Kentucky Fried Movie, National Lampoon's Animal House, The Blues Brothers, Trading Places, Spies Like Us, Three Amigos,* and *Coming to America.* What Landis is perhaps most famous for is the segment in *The Twilight Zone: The Movie* in which he ordered a helicopter too close to his actors, just before the helicopter lost control, killing Vic Morrow and two children. Landis bought the former Rock Hudson estate at 9402 Beverly Crest Drive. Hudson died in the house in 1985, becoming the first celebrity known to have died of AIDS.

Another public figure who lives off Coldwater Canyon is former Columbia Pictures president and now independent producer, Dawn Steel, who was pictured on the December 1988 cover of *California* magazine for being one of the worst bosses in California. The magazine, which wrote that

"Steel's snits and verbal abusiveness are the stuff of legend in an industry in which the ability to act like a ten-year-old bully is viewed as a mark of professionalism," repeated a story that Steel supposedly once told a prospective employee: "'Look, I've gone through hundreds of secretaries . . . I'm hard on them. The last one left just because I called her a c***. Would that be a problem for you?' The woman reportedly said yes and left." (Steel's defenders were quick to point out that she is no meaner than any of Hollywood's top male bosses. *Top Gun* producer Don Simpson, Disney production chief Jeffrey 'Beat 'em Up' Katzenberg and former Fox Chairman Barry "Killer" Diller were cited as the toughest people to work for.)

Perhaps the biggest surprise celebrity resident of this area is Watergate conspirator John Dean. Dean, a former aide to President Nixon, implicated Nixon in the cover-up and was the man primarily responsible for bringing down the Nixon presidency.

14. HOME ONCE OWNED BY DAVID O. SELZNICK AND LATER BY ED McMAHON, 1050 Summit Drive (corner of Cove)

This mansion, originally built in the 1930s for *Gone With the Wind* producer, David O. Selznick, and his wife Irene Mayer, has had a succession of celebrity owners, including Sammy Davis, Jr. (who later moved a block away); producer Freddie Fields; and Johnny Carson's sidekick Ed McMahon. McMahon sold it in 1991 for $4.1 million as part of his divorce settlement from his wife, Victoria.

15. CHARLIE CHAPLIN'S "BREAKWAY" HOME, 1085 Summit Drive (corner of Cove)

Chaplin's two-story Spanish-style mansion, built in 1922, became famous because everything inside used to fall apart. "To save money on its construction," Charles Lockwood wrote in *Dream Palaces*, an intriguing book about the mansions of Beverly Hills, Chaplin "used studio carpenters when they weren't busy making sets. This seemed like a sensible plan, but it turned out to be a mistake. His carpenters had become so accustomed to putting together temporary sets that they had forgotten how to build a permanent structure. No sooner had Charlie moved into his new house than little things began to go wrong. Paneling split. Ornamental trim fell to the floors. Doors came loose on their hinges. Floors started to squeak. To Charlie's chagrin, his friends and neighbors began calling his Summit Drive dream palace 'Breakaway House.'"

After Chaplin sold the house in 1950, it passed through several hands, and at one point was owned by actor George Hamilton, who, according to some, served as a front man for his friends, the Marcoses of the Philippines. Hamilton later sold the house to former Saudi arms dealer Adnan Khashoggi's daughter. In 1991 the Republic of the Philippines successfully sued to get title of the house, which was recently listed for sale at $5 million.

16. PICKFAIR, 1143 Summit Drive

Pickfair was the most famous house in Hollywood in the 1920s and 1930s, when it was owned by superstars Mary Pickford and Douglas Fairbanks, Sr. Charles Lockwood, in *Dream Palaces*, noted that even though "other stars' dream palaces would be architecturally more distinguished, more expensive, and even larger than Pickfair . . . no one star's home ever claimed the same feverish public devotion year after year. Douglas Fairbanks and Mary Pickford were two of Hollywood's biggest and most enduring stars, and they were the nation's most popular couple. Pickfair was the most famous house in America, even more famous than the White House. More Americans cared about what happened there than at Warren G. Harding or Calvin Coolidge's White House."

After the couple divorced in 1936, Fairbanks moved out, and Pickford's next husband, Buddy Rogers, moved in. According to Pickford's biographer Scott Eyeman, Pickford tried "to donate the property to a charity, university or hospital after her death, but the $300,000 - $400,000 yearly upkeep dissuaded those who were approached." Rogers lived there until her death in 1979, and the house was sold to Los Angeles Lakers' owner, Jerry Buss, for $5,362,000. Buss, in turn, sold the 42-room mansion to singer Pia Zadora and her multimillionaire husband, Meshulam Riklis, for just under $7 million. Pia promptly demolished Pickfair, much to the horror of Beverly Hills preservationists. A new three-story mansion is being built on the site. It will be one of at least five houses Pia and her husband own in the area.

17. LAST HOME OF SAMMY DAVIS, JR., 1151
Summit Drive (across from Pickfair)

(DIRECTIONS: Bear left around Pickfair. Ignore the street sign, which will only confuse you—Summit turns into Pickfair—and then make a left onto San Ysidro Drive.)

18. LAST HOME OF FRED ASTAIRE, 1155 San Ysidro Drive
Go slowly or you will miss it. Astaire's was the first home on your right.

19. LAST HOME OF DANNY KAYE, 1103 San Ysidro Drive
Further down the street; before the intersection of San Ysidro and Tower Road.

(DIRECTIONS: Make a right turn onto Tower Road. Just after 1122 Tower Road, you will come to a three-way intersection with Tower Lane on the left, Tower Grove Drive straight ahead, and Tower Road on the right. Tower Lane is a private road on which Bruce Springsteen has a $13.9 million estate; it is not visible from the street.

Tower Grove features an extraordinary French chateau at 1400 Tower Grove, which was once the site of a house owned by a succession of entertainment figures, including David O. Selznick and Elton John, and some historically interesting houses such as the site of John Barrymore's home, Bella Vista, which was also later lived in by Katherine Hepburn, Marlon Brando, and Candice Bergen. Unfortunately, from this direction, Tower Grove is reachable only by negotiating a very steep mountainous road. The road is guaranteed to make even the most experienced driver skip a few heartbeats.

Unless you are absolutely determined to see alleged madam Heidi Fleiss' former home at 1270 Tower Grove Dr., you are probably better off making a right turn onto Tower Road, which dead-ends at the top of a hill which is much easier to negotiate. At the end of Tower Road you can make a U-turn at the cul-de-sac and continue down Tower until you reach Benedict Canyon.)

20-22. CELEBRITY HOMES ON TOWER ROAD

Jack Lemmon lives at 1143 Tower Road; Jay Leno lived at 1151; and Sid Sheinberg, the president and chief operating officer of MCA (Universal Studios' parent company) lives in the former Spencer Tracy estate at 1158 Tower Road.

(DIRECTIONS: After touring Tower Road and turning around you will reach Benedict Canyon. At this point you can either make a right turn and see Harold Lloyd's estate, Green Acres: what you can see of the Manson murder site, and the house that George "Superman" Reeves died in; and then make a U-turn again. Or you can skip these houses and make a left turn from Tower Road and proceed to the David Geffen's $47.5 million mansion, and then proceed to Roxbury Drive, where Lucille Ball and other celebrities lived. The following descriptions should help you decide which option to choose.)

23. GREEN ACRES, 1740 Green Acres Drive

This 48,000 square-foot mansion, complete with 44 rooms and 26 bathrooms, was sold by producer and Marshall Field heir Ted Field in 1993 for nearly $18 million. From the street all you can see are one of the twelve fountains. Not visible are the twelve formal gardens, the 120-foot-long cascading waterfall, the Olympic-size swimming pool, and the 800-foot-long canoe pond lake near the 9-hole golf course (which is adjacent to the 9-hole golf course on the former Jack Warner estate. The two courses were sometimes combined whenever the owners wanted to play a full 18 holes.) Green Acres was built by silent film star Harold Lloyd, who lived in the mansion for more than 40 years until his death in 1971.

24. SITE OF THE CHARLES MANSON CULT MURDER, 10050 Cielo Drive

One of the most savage and well publicized murders ever committed in the United States occurred here on the early morning hours of August 9, 1969. Four members of Charles Manson's cult cut telephone lines, climbed a rocky hillside, broke into the main house and slaughtered actress Sharon Tate (who was eight and a half months pregnant with director Roman Polanski's baby); coffee heiress Abigail Folger; Folger's lover, producer Wojtek Frykowski; internationally known hair stylist Jay Sebring; and Steven Parent, an 18-year-old college student who happened to be visiting the estate's caretaker. Tate was stabbed 16 times, and Frykowski 51 times. The murderers wrote the word ''Pig'' on the wall of the house with the victims' blood.

Manson supposedly ordered his cult followers to kill the house's occupants because he wanted to terrify Doris Day's son, record producer Terry Melcher, whom Manson had asked to help further his (Manson's) recording career. Until a few months before the slaughter, Melcher had lived in the house with his then-girlfriend Candice Bergen. After Melcher moved out, Tate and her husband director, Roman Polanski, rented the house.

Even today, the murder is relived on television tabloid shows, and Manson is held up as an example of Evil personified. The house, high on the hill, is not visible from the street, but you can see the hillside Manson's followers had to scale in order to reach their victims.

The home where the Manson cult killed actress Sharon Tate and four others.

25. FALCON LAIR, 1436 Bella Drive

Falcon Lair was Rudolph Valentino's hideaway and was named for a never-filmed screenplay, *The Hooded Falcon,* written for him by his second wife, Natacha Rambova. According to John Pashdag, author of *Hollywoodland USA:* "When Valentino bought the house in 1925, his popularity was such that the high wall alone couldn't keep out the female fans, so the screen's first great Latin lover added floodlights, guards, and a half a dozen dogs, including three Great Danes and two mastiffs, to keep his admirers at bay." Since 1953 Falcon Lair has been owned by Doris Duke, who is one of the richest women in the world. Her father, James Duke, organized the American Tobacco Company (now American Brands, Inc.).

26. "SUPERMAN" DEATH HOUSE, 1579 Benedict Canyon Drive

George Reeves, who was television's "Superman" from 1952 to 1957, was found dead in his home in the early hours of June 16, 1959, with a .30 caliber Luger by his side. His death was officially ruled a suicide; however, his mother never accepted the official ruling and hired private detectives in an unsuccessful attempt to prove he was murdered. Some writers later claimed that Reeves' ghost haunts the house. The fact that a subsequent owner, screenwriter/director Phil Robinson, was inspired here to write the ghost story, *Field of Dreams,* is probably just a coincidence.

OTHER CELEBRITIES WHO LIVE ON BENE-
DICT CANYON: Mickey Rourke, Darren McGa-
vin, Alan Carr, Elizabeth Montgomery, Mac-
Donald Carey, Jacqueline Bisset, Belinda Carlisle,
Anna Maria Albergetti, Julia Phillips, Ed Zwick,
Gene Simmons and Shannon Tweed, Donna Mills,
Ann-Margret and Roger Smith, Eddie Murphy, and
Hugh O'Brien. Unfortunately, virtually all of these
houses are not visible from the street, which is
why no organized tour covers the street. Also not
visible from the street—and behind gates—is a
$3.5 million house at 2570 Benedict Canyon that
"Roseanne" star Roseanne Barr Arnold and her
husband, Tom, leased from CBS Records executive, Spencer Proffer, and which Proffer claimed
the Arnolds damaged to the tune of $205,000. The
Arnolds denied turning the house into a pigsty and
counterclaimed that they were framed by *National
Enquirer* reporters who entered the house after the
Arnolds vacated the premises and destroyed property and stole household items themselves so the
Enquirer could write a story. The Arnolds dropped
their lawsuit against the tabloid. Proffer later
dropped his lawsuit and apologized to the Arnolds,
lending credence to the Arnolds' claim that they
were set up. Several celebrities also live on the
many side streets off Benedict Canyon, including
Richard Dawson, Rod McKuen, Robert Loggia,
Tom Snyder, Joel Schumacher, Stephanie Powers,
Barry Bostwick, Angelica Huston, Mary Frann,
Rita Rudner, and Carrie Fisher.

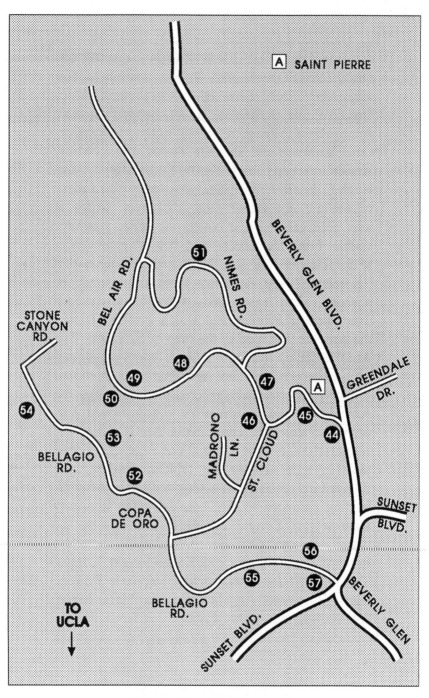

MAP 5 BEL - AIR

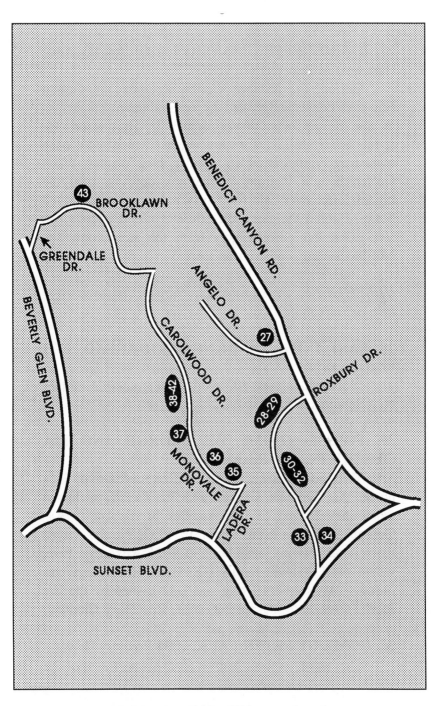

MAP 4 BEVERLY HILLS

27. DAVID GEFFEN MANSION, 1801 Angelo Drive
(just west of Benedict Canyon)

Geffen, the head of Geffen Records and Geffen Films, is consistently rated by entertainment magazines as one of the most powerful men in Hollywood. He spent $47.5 million for this estate, which was once owned by Warner Bros. co-founder, Jack Warner. When Geffen bought it from Warner's widow he paid the highest price ever paid for a private home in the United States. Behind the gates, the house reportedly looks like Versailles, but unfortunately from the street, only the half-block-long walls can be seen.

(DIRECTIONS: From Benedict Canyon, make a right turn onto Roxbury Drive.)

28. LAST HOME OF AGNES MOORHEAD, 1023 Roxbury Drive

Moorhead played Elizabeth Montgomery's mother on "Bewitched."

29. FORMER HOME OF GEORGE AND IRA GERSHWIN, 1019 Roxbury Drive

Two doors down, at 1019 Roxbury Drive, is a house that lyricists George and Ira Gershwin leased when they moved to Los Angeles in the late 1930s. George died of a brain tumor in 1937, but Ira stayed there, until moving next door to 1021 Roxbury Drive, where the Gershwin family's Roxbury Recordings was based. 1019 Roxbury Drive was later owned by the late José Ferrer and his former wife, Rosemary Clooney.

30. HOME OF PETER FALK, 1004 Roxbury Drive

The actor is best known for his portrayal of the

Los Angeles police detective, Lieutenant Columbo. His portrayal has earned him four Emmy Awards.

31. FORMER HOME OF JACK BENNY, 1002 Roxbury Drive

Jack Benny lived next door to Falk's current residence for almost thirty years. In 1966 he moved into an apartment, and then to his last residence, a mansion across from the Playboy Mansion (p. 54).

Lucy's house on Roxbury Drive.

32. LAST HOME OF LUCILLE BALL, 1000 Roxbury Drive (corner of Lexington)

Lucy paid $85,500 for this five-bedroom house in 1955. After she died in 1989, the home was put on the market for $7.8 million. The house was subsequently marked down several times and now lists for $3.75 million.

33. FORMER HOME OF RICK SCHRODER, 921 Roxbury Drive

The former star of "Silver Spoons," now lives in a ranch in Colorado with his wife Andrea.

34. HOME OF JIMMY STEWART, 918 Roxbury Drive

(DIRECTIONS: At the end of the block is Sunset Boulevard. Make a right turn onto Sunset and continue west for about half a mile. Make a right onto Ladera Drive, and an immediate left onto Monovale Drive.)

35. HOME AT 120 MONOVALE DRIVE (corner of Ladera and Monovale Drives)

This was Frank Sinatra and Mia Farrow's honeymoon home. They lived here for a short time in 1966.

36. ELVIS PRESLEY'S LAST LOS ANGELES HOME, 144 Monovale Drive

Elvis lived here, next door to 120 Monovale Drive, from December 1967 to March 1975, when he sold the house to "Kojak" star Telly Savalas. (Savalas now lives at the Universal Sheraton Hotel.) About all that is visible from the street is Elvis' balcony.

37. FORMER BURT REYNOLDS/LONI ANDERSON HOME, 245 Monovale Drive

Reynolds and Anderson lived here until 1990, when they moved to his home in Florida. When he began working on the television program "Evening Shade," they subsequently moved back to Los Angeles and rented a home on Mulholland Drive for $40,000 a month.

Tourists may be more impressed with the two houses next door, owned by ordinary multimillionaires, at 265 and 275 Monovale Drive. These houses sport some of the most modern statues in the city.

(Note: In what seems like a conspiracy to confuse tourists, Monovale changes its name and becomes Carolwood Drive at this point.)

38-42. "CELEBRITY ROW": 301 TO 375 CAROLWOOD DRIVE

Celebrities seem to cluster along the rest of this block. One of Barbra Streisand's six Los Angeles-area homes is at 301 Carolwood. (She also owns four houses in one compound in Ramirez Canyon in Malibu, which she has been trying to unload for years.) A noncelebrity lives at 325 Carolwood, but next door to that—at 355 Carolwood—is Walt Disney's widow. Walt lived there until his death in 1966. Next door to Mrs. Disney—at 375 Carolwood—is the home of Gregory Peck. At the end of the block—at 391 Carolwood, where the Dobermans bark the loudest and the barbed wire looks the most menacing—is Rod Stewart's former home. In 1992 the popular rock star moved to a gated community on Mulholland Drive, and put the house up for sale. The asking price was $10 million.

(DIRECTIONS: Make a left at Brooklawn Drive and proceed 1/10 of a mile.)

43. "THE COLBYS" MANSION, 1060 Brooklawn Drive
The exterior of this house, owned by Hilton Hotels CEO Barron Hilton, was used as "The Colbys" residence in the "Dynasty" spin-off of that name. The house is not visible from the street.

(DIRECTIONS: Brooklawn changes its name to North Faring. As you continue, you will see on your left Harvard/Westlake School, an exclusive private prepatory school which counts among its graduates Candice Bergen, Shirley Temple, Tracy Nelson and June Lockhart. Tuition for the 1993—1994 school year was $10,900. At the stop sign, make a right turn at Greendale Drive. Then make a left onto Beverly Glen Boulevard, and an immediate right at St. Pierre Road.)

44. ONE-TIME RESIDENCE OF JOHNNY "TARZAN" WEISMULLER, 488 St. Pierre Road
The entire house is encircled by a swimming pool which resembles a moat.

45. FORMER "MAMAS AND THE PAPAS" PARTY HOUSE, 414 St. Pierre Road
In 1972 Mick Jagger needed an L.A. base to rehearse for a U.S. tour and rented this house on the recommendation of John Phillips of The Mamas and The Papas. Later, Phillips rented it himself and hosted

some wild parties for his friends.

In his autobiography *Papa John*, Phillips admitted he was evicted for nonpayment of rent.

(Note: St. Pierre changes its name to St. Cloud Road here.)

46. FORMER HOME OF SONNY AND CHER, 364 St. Cloud Road

In the 1991 remake of *Father of the Bride*, Steve Martin had some comic scenes here when he sneaked into his wealthy in-laws' study and tried to see their bankbook. In real life the estate was once owned by Sonny and Cher and later by *Hustler* magazine publisher, Larry Flynt.

47. FORMER JOHNNY CARSON HOME, 400 St. Cloud Road

Carson bought this house in 1972 from Mervyn LeRoy, the director of *The Wizard of Oz*, and lived here until 1983. It is now occupied by Carson's ex-wife number three, Joanna.

(DIRECTIONS: Bear to the left when you reach the intersection without a sign.)

48. RONALD REAGAN'S RETIREMENT HOME, 668 St. Cloud Road

Reagan's wealthy friends bought this house for him before he left office and gave him a three-year lease with an option to buy. The address was originally 666 St. Cloud, but Nancy Reagan, perhaps after consulting with her astrologer, had the house number changed to 668. 666 is the Sign of the Beast in the Book of Revelations in the New Testament.

(Note: St. Cloud changes names and becomes Bel Air Road without warning.)

49. "BEVERLY HILLBILLIES" MANSION, 750 Bel Air Road

Adjacent to the Reagans' is the house that Jed Clampett and his family called home in "The Beverly Hillbillies," the enormously popular television show that aired from 1962 to 1970. The mansion was once known as the Kirkeby Estate, and was considered to be one of the great estates of Beverly Hills until it was bought in 1986 by Hollywood dealmaker Jerrold Perrenchio, a former agent of Liz Taylor and Marlon Brando and former partner of television producer, Norman Lear. Perrenchio, whose net worth was estimated by *Forbes* magazine to be around $665 million, paid $13.6 million for the mansion, dismantled it, and bought the three neighboring properties for an additional $9 million, in order to build a what one writer called "what by all accounts looks to be a modern monument to himself."

50. ANOTHER FORMER "MAMAS AND THE PAPAS" HOUSE, 783 Bel Air Road (corner of Strada Vecchia)

John and Michelle Phillips of The Mamas and the Papas leased this home across the street from the "Beverly Hillbillies" mansion for three years in the late 1960s before moving to the one at 414 St. Pierre Road. Previous owners include Jeanette MacDonald and Nelson Eddy.

(DIRECTIONS: At the intersection of Bel Air Road and Nimes Road, you can either turn left and see Alfred

An aerial view of "The Beverly Hillbillies" house (top) and Ronald Reagan's retirement home next door.

Hitchcock's last home at 910 Bel Air Road, Zsa Zsa Gabor's home at 1001 Bel Air Road—which, incidentally, was also Howard Hughes' last Los Angeles home—and Art Linkletter's home at 1100 Bel Air Road. Or, you can make a right turn at the intersection and see:)

51. HOME OF ELIZABETH TAYLOR, 700 Nimes Road

Taylor, who has overcome most of her additions—except her addiction to publicity—lives here, just up the street from Burt Bacharach, who lives at 658 Nimes Road, and Mac Davis, who lives at 759 Nimes Road. (Jack Ryan, the inventor of the Barbie doll, lived at 688 Nimes Road, a home built for 1930s silent screen star Warren Baxter.)

(DIRECTIONS: Proceed south on Nimes and bear left onto St. Cloud. You will pass 400 and 364 St. Cloud again, as well as 322 St. Cloud, which was once owned by Louis B. Mayer and later by Jerry Lewis. Just past Madrono Lane, you will see a sign pointing toward the Hotel Bel-Air. The street name is not visible, but that street is Copa De Oro Road. Make a right turn onto Copa De Oro. A block away you will see another sign announcing Amapola Lane. Look to your right. The mammoth white colonial at 420 Amapola Lane is owned by comedian Bob Newhart. Continue on Copa De Oro Road.)

52. HOME OF TOM JONES, 363 Copa De Oro Road

The singer lives in this red-brick home once owned by Dean Martin, directly across the street from 362 Copa De Oro, the home of Jerome Moss (the M of

A & M Records).

(DIRECTIONS: Make a right turn onto Bellagio Road and then another right onto Stone Canyon Road. On your left you will see Bellagio Road again. Two houses down is 10615 Bellagio Road, the last home of "Star Trek" creator Gene Roddenberry. Cary Grant also lived in that house at one point. You can make a quick left to see the house, but to continue the tour you want to keep heading north on Stone Canyon to the Hotel Bel-Air.)

53. FORMER GREER GARSON ESTATE, 680 Stone Canyon Road

Garson, a popular actress in the 1940s, won an Academy Award for her role in *Mrs. Miniver* and was nominated for best actress on six other occasions.

54. HOTEL BEL-AIR, 701 Stone Canyon Road, (310) 472-1211, (800) 648-4097

Everyone raves about the Hotel Bel-Air. Charles Moore, Peter Becker, and Regula Campbell, in their guide to Los Angeles' architectural highlights, *The City Observed,* call it "one of the most wonderful places in Southern California." *Conde Nast Traveler* and *USA Today* both rate it as the best hotel in the United States. Gault Millau's *The Best of Los Angeles* gushes: "If Sleeping Beauty were to wake up in Southern California, no doubt she'd find herself in the enchanted gardens of the Hotel Bel-Air. The grounds are so beautiful that they almost seem to be a fairy-tale parody. You will be charmed by the swans, the ancient trees, the eleven acres of private park, the welcoming reception with its crackling fire and the quasi-country-chateau architecture." You will also be impressed with the celebrities you will see at the hotel. It is one of the best places in town to see celebrities, visiting European royalty, and traveling industry leaders.

(DIRECTIONS: After leaving the hotel, make a left turn and head south toward Sunset. Stone Canyon leads to Sunset; however, you do not want to go that far since you can only make a right turn at Sunset, which is a very busy street. About 3/10 of a mile past the Hotel Bel-Air, you will reach Bellagio Road again. Make a left, heading east on Bellagio Road. The street signs here are very confusing, so make sure you follow the sign that reads "Sunset Boulevard East," and bear right for a block where you will see a sign announcing the 300 block of Copa De Oro Road. Go on Copa De Oro Road for a block, then make a left at the sign that reads 10400 Bellagio Road.)

55. FORMER BRIAN WILSON AND EDGAR RICE BURROUGHS HOUSE, 10452 Bellagio Road
Brian Wilson of the Beach Boys bought this Mediterranean villa, once owned by Edgar Rice Burroughs, in the 1960s, and painted it purple, upsetting the neighborhood homeowners' association to no end.

56. "9 TO 5" FILMING SITE, 10431 Bellagio Road
According to John Pashdag, author of *Hollywoodland USA*, this was "Dabney Coleman's house in *9 to 5*, where Jane Fonda, Dolly Parton, and Lily Tomlin tied up their no-good boss, and hung him from the ceiling."

57. HOME AT 10410 BELLAGIO ROAD
Home of Los Angeles Rams' owner Georgia Frontiere.

48

OTHER CELEBRITIES WHO LIVE IN BEL-AIR: Leonard Nimoy, Kareem Abdul-Jabbar, Tim Mathieson, Christina Ferrare, James Caan, Ted Bessel, Red Buttons, Jaclyn Smith, Alan Alda, Michael J. Fox, Lionel Richie, Judith Krantz, Dave Winfield, Frank Robinson, Lindsay Buckingham, Quincy Jones, David Wolper, Merv Adelson, Jane Wyatt, David Murdoch, Neil Simon, Dick Martin, Harvey Korman, Gene Wilder, Martha Raye, Della Reese, Don Simpson, Michael Eisner, Robert Stack, and Moon Unit Zappa. Some tours point out a home on Sunset Boulevard as belonging to Joanne Carson, Johnny's second wife (Truman Capote died in her house). Carson does live on Sunset Boulevard, but she lives in Brentwood, west of UCLA, not in Bel-Air. Former Bel-Air residents include Joan Rivers, Henry Fonda, and Judy Garland.

(DIRECTIONS: Make a right turn onto Bel Air Road, which will take you to the east gate of the community of Bel-Air. You should recognize the gates; it has been on television often enough. You may have seen it in the opening credits of "The Rockford Files." Continue straight across Sunset Boulevard, where the street changes its name to Beverly Glen. You are now in Holmby Hills, a neighborhood that is even more expensive than Beverly Hills and Bel-Air. Take Beverly Glen Boulevard south for about half a mile; and then by the park—Holmby Park—make a left onto Club View Drive. The first house on left is the talk of Los Angeles.)

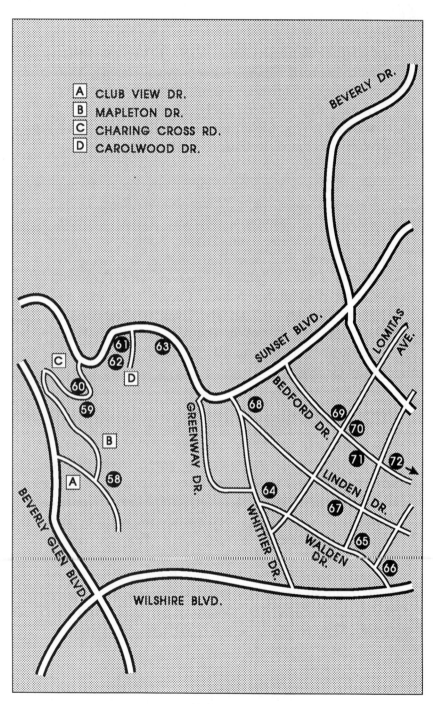

MAP 6 BEVERLY HILLS

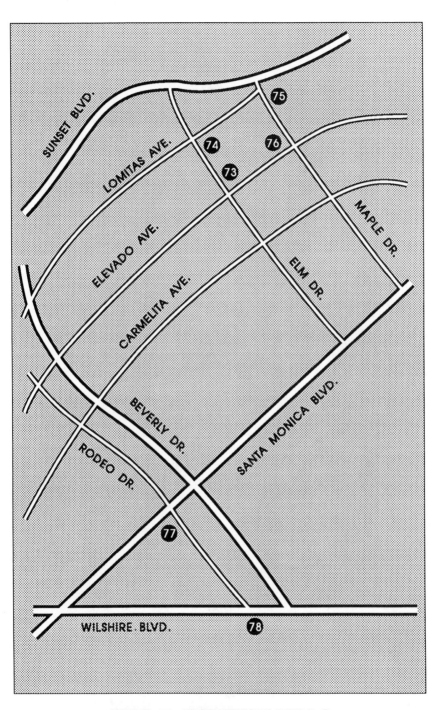

MAP 7   BEVERLY HILLS

Producer Aaron Spelling's home is the largest and most extravagant private residence in Los Angeles.

58. AARON SPELLING'S CHATEAU, 594 N. Mapleton Drive (corner of Club View)

Comedian David Steinberg once remarked: "In Hollywood, there's the rich. And then there's Aaron Spelling." Spelling is not a household name, even though he was honored in the *Guinness Book of World Records* for being the most prolific producer of television programs of all time. Spelling is the man responsible for "The Mod Squad," "Charlie's Angels," "Fantasy Island," "The Love Boat," "Starsky and Hutch," "The Rookies," "Hart to Hart," "Hotel," "T. J. Hooker," "Vegas," "Dynasty," and more recently "Beverly Hills 90210." He once told an interviewer the reason he is so successful is because he gives people what they want: "escape from the harshness of day-to-day life."

In 1983 Spelling bought the old Bing Crosby estate, tore it down, and built a six-acre, 123-room mansion that is reportedly as large as a football field, or 31 times the size of the average American home. The *Los Angeles Herald Examiner* placed the 56,000-square-foot chateau in perspective by noting it was smaller than the Pentagon, but larger than the Taj Mahal, Disney's largest soundstage, or George Washington's Mt. Vernon home. The dressing room and closets of Spelling's wife, Candy take up an entire wing. Even some of Spelling's neighbors think the size of the house is obscene. Not counting the household help, four people live in this house: Aaron, Candy, their son Randy, and their daughter Tori, who plays ditzy Donna on "Beverly Hills 90210."

(DIRECTIONS: After ooh-ing and aah-ing the Spelling Manor, continue north on Mapleton Drive, passing

Charing Cross Road, until you see 232 S. Mapleton Drive. That is the former home of Humphrey Bogart and Lauren Bacall, now owned by producer Ray Stark. Make a U-turn as soon as possible and go left onto Charing Cross Road.)

59. THE PLAYBOY MANSION, 10236 Charing Cross Road

Hefner lives and works out of his six-acre estate, which he purchased in 1971.

60. FORMER JACK BENNY ESTATE, 10231 Charing Cross Road

The comedian lived here, in this house directly across the street from the Playboy Mansion, from 1965 until his death in 1974. The house is now owned by psychologist, author *(Nice Girls Do)*, and television personality, Irene Kassorla, and her husband Norman Friedman, the president of Daisy Systems Corporation.

(DIRECTIONS: Make a right onto Sunset, and proceed 2/10 of mile to Carolwood Drive.)

61. JAYNE MANSFIELD'S "PINK PALACE," 10100 Sunset Boulevard

This pink 18-room mansion, now owned by Englebert Humperdinck, was originally built by Rudy Vallee and was later owned by sex symbol Jayne Mansfield. Charles Lockwood, in his book *Dream Palaces,* reports that "although Jayne may have looked and acted the part of the dumb blonde, in remodeling the Pink Palace she knew how to get the most for her money. Her Hungarian muscleman husband, Mickey Hargitay, had been a builder, and he completed or supervised most of the work. Then Jayne's press agent, Jim Byron, asked fifteen hundred furniture and building supply houses for free samples. Think of the honor, he told them, of having your—fill in the blank—as part of the Pink Palace. The pitch worked. Jayne received over a hundred fifty thousand dollars' worth of free merchandise.''

The Playboy Mansion.

62. OWLWOOD, 141 S. Carolwood Drive

This house, directly behind Humperdinck's on the cul-de-sac south of Sunset, had a succession of celebrity owners: Sonny and Cher, Tony Curtis, and 20th Century Fox co-founder Joseph Schenck. Marilyn Monroe lived here in 1949 when she was Schenck's mistress.

63. HADERWAY HALL, 10000 Sunset Boulevard

The lifelike sculptures in front of this estate have always intrigued tourists. One of the pieces—a couple with binoculars trying to see what is in the house—leads one to ask if anyone famous ever lived here. The answer is yes. Judy Garland rented the property in 1948, and two years later, when she was separated from her second husband, director Vincente Minnelli, she recuperated from a suicide attempt here. The statue of a cop giving a ticket to trespassers at the front gate should be self-explanatory, but one can only guess at what the statues of the two naked boys trying to peer over the fence, next to the security cameras, are supposed to represent.

(DIRECTIONS: Continue east on Sunset Boulevard for two blocks and make a right turn onto Greenway Drive, where you will see some of the prettiest lawns on the tour. You are now back in Beverly Hills. You will pass Steve Lawrence and Edie Gorme's home at 820 Greenway Drive, and a house at 813 Greenway that Debbie Reynolds' once owned, and where her daughter Carrie Fisher grew up. Blake Edwards later used the house for a scene in his movie S.O.B. in which Richard Mulligan crashed a car into the kitchen. Edwards liked the house so much that he and his wife Julie Andrews later bought it. The Edwardses now live in Brentwood.

At the stop sign make a right turn onto Whittier Drive.
Just past the sign on your right that reads Walden Drive
is a house on the left side of the three-way corner of
Whittier Drive, Lomitas Avenue and Walden Drive. That
is Buddy Hackett's house, and you will want to bear left
on Walden after his house.)

64. HOME OF BUDDY HACKETT, 800 Whittier Drive

The white elephant in front of his house was reportedly given to him as a gift by his friend Sammy Davis, Jr.

65. HOUSE AT 614 N. WALDEN DRIVE

Several blocks down the street is a house you might recognize from *Beverly Hills Cop II*. Eddie Murphy pretended to be a Beverly Hills building inspector, sent the workmen remodeling it packing, and moved in himself. He told his friends on the Beverly Hills police force that it was his uncle's house.

66. THE WITCH'S HOUSE, 516 N. Walden Drive (corner of Carmelita)

This is perhaps the most unusual house on the tour of Beverly Hills. It looks like the witch's house in "Hansel and Gretel," and although the Beverly Hills Historical Society reports it has not appeared in any famous films, it did appear in some silent films in the 1920s, when the house served as an office for Irvin C. Willat Productions, a movie studio in Culver City. When the studio was sold in 1926, a former owner transplated the house and moved it to the heart of Beverly Hills. The current owners, an elderly couple, had the house on the market a few years ago, and want the house preserved.

The Witch's House in Beverly Hills.

(DIRECTIONS: At the corner of Walden, make left onto Carmelita Avenue, and another left onto Linden Drive.)

67. HOME OF DAVID BEGELMAN, 705 Linden Drive

Begelman is the former head of Columbia Pictures who was convicted in 1978 of embezzlement. He had forged his signature on several checks, including the one which proved to be his undoing: it was a $10,000 check with actor Cliff Robertson's name on it. The scandal, which was chronicled in David McClintock's bestseller *Indecent Exposure,* did not end Begelman's movie career. He went on to head MGM productions and Gladden Pictures and produced *Weekend at Bernie's, Wisdom,* and *The Fabulous Baker Boys.* (When you see his unusually trimmed hedges you might also think of *Edward Scissorshands.* Begelman had nothing to do with that movie.)

68. "BUGSY" SIEGEL MURDER SITE, 810 Linden Drive

Benjamin "Bugsy" Siegel—the gangster whom J. Edgar Hoover once called "the most dangerous man in America"—was murdered here in a home leased by his mistress, Virginia Hill. The 41-year-old Siegel was shot shortly before midnight on June 20, 1947, reportedly because the Mafia suspected he was skimming money he had borrowed from them to build the Flamingo Hotel in Las Vegas. Besides being the subject of a 1991 movie starring Warren Beatty and Annette Bening, Siegel's main claim to fame was that he reportedly convinced organized crime to build the first luxury hotel in Las Vegas, where gambling was legal. Some say that Las Vegas was built largely as a consequence of Bugsy's vision. In Los Angeles he ran most of the mob's gambling and prostitution operations and socialized with movie stars like George Raft. *Time* magazine called him "perhaps the most famous mobster of his era." (Note: The producers of *Bugsy* were not able to get permission to use this house in the movie. The Virginia Hill house seen in the movie is located in Hancock Park.)

The Beverly Hills home in which mobster Bugsy Siegel was killed.

(DIRECTIONS: At the end of Linden Drive, make a right onto Sunset Boulevard, and then another right onto Bedford Drive.)

69. "DOWN AND OUT IN BEVERLY HILLS" HOME, 802 N. Bedford Drive

This was the house in which Richard Dreyfuss and Bette Midler lived in *Down and Out in Beverly Hills*. (The inside of the house and the backyard pool area were actually recreated on the Disney back lot.)

70. FORMER HOME OF LANA TURNER, 730 N. Bedford Drive

It was here, in 1958, that Lana's teenage daughter, Cheryl Crane, stabbed to death Lana's lover, gangster Johnny Stompanato (alias Johnny Valentine).

71. HOME OF COMEDIAN STEVE MARTIN, 721 N. Bedford Drive

72. ONE-TIME HOME OF "THE IT GIRL," CLARA BOW, 512 N. Bedford Drive

Bow was considered the Madonna of her day (the Roaring '20s) and had quite a wild reputation. One of Hollywood's favorite legends is that she was so promiscuous that she had sex with the entire starting lineup of the USC football team. Her principal biographer, David Stenn, however, disputes the story. In *Clara Bow: Runnin' Wild,* Stenn writes that Clara was just an avid football fan who used to invite the USC players and their opponents to parties at her house after the games on Saturday nights. The parties were also attended by her actress friends, including Joan Crawford. Lowry McCaslin, a sophomore end for the team, was quoted as saying: "We had a good time, but it wasn't that exciting."

(DIRECTIONS: After viewing Bow's house, make a right turn onto Carmelita Avenue. To see the next major concentration of show-business homes, pass Camden, Rodeo, Beverly, Cañon, Crescent, Rexford, Alpine, and Foothill Drives, until you reach Elm Drive. It should be

noted in passing, though, that each of these streets has
something to offer of interest. For example, a right on
Bedford Drive will take you to The Church of the Good
Shepherd at 505 N. Bedford Drive, where funeral servies
were held for Alfred Hitchcock and Rudolph Valentino,
Rod Stewart married Rachel Hunter, and Elizabeth
Taylor married the first of her eight husbands. A left
onto Rodeo Drive will take you to Gene Kelly and Carl
Reiner's homes at 714 and 725 Rodeo Drive, respec-
tively. Rodeo Drive going south leads to the world-
famous shopping district, usually referred to as Rodeo
Drive. A right on either Crescent or Rexford, going
south, leads to the magnificent Beverly Hills City Hall.
Alpine is the street that comedian Phil Silvers lived on;
and Jackie Collins and Richard Benjamin live on
Foothill Drive.)

73. FORMER HOME OF IVAN REITMAN, 704 N. Elm Drive

Reitman has produced and directed numerous blockbluster comedies including *Kindergarten Cop, Ghostbusters, Ghostbusters II, Twins, Legal Eagles, Meatballs* and *Stripes.*

74. REAL LIFE "NIGHTMARE ON ELM DRIVE" HOME, 722 N. Elm Drive

One of Hollywood's most notorious murders occurred here on the night of August 20, 1989, when José Menendez, the 45-year-old chairman of Live Entertainment, a division of Carolco Pictures, and his 44-year-old wife, Kitty, were found brutally slain in their family room. Their faces had been blown off by repeated shotgun blasts. Police at first believed that the Menendezes might have been killed by mobsters (as you may have noticed, there are quite a few in this town). However, several months later, the Menendezes' two sons, Lyle and Erik, were arrested after allegedly telling their celebrity psychiatrist, Jerome Oziel, that they killed their parents. The boys had allegedly threatened to kill Oziel if he told anybody, and Oziel, who was concerned for his own safety, had his patient (she also claims to be his former lover) Judalon Smyth eavesdrop on the therapy sessions. Smyth took it upon herself to report the murders to the police.

It turned out that Erik had, with a friend, earlier written a screenplay about wealthy 18-year-olds who murder their parents for money, and that both boys had gone on a $700,000 shopping binge shortly after the murders. As this book goes to press, Erik and Lyle await trial.

The house, which had been rented previously to Elton John, Prince, and Hal Prince, was sold to an unidentified investor in 1991 for $3.56 million, which is less than the $4 million the Menendezes paid for it in 1988.

75. HOME OF GEORGE BURNS, 720 N. Maple Drive
The facade of Burns' home was used in "The George Burns and Gracie Allen Show."

76. FORMER HOME OF DIANA ROSS, 701 N. Maple Drive
The current owner, James Burrows, is the co-creator and co-producer of "Cheers." (Maple Drive seems to attract quite a few celebrities. Gene Barry, Valerie Harper and "Love Connection" creator Eric Lieber all live on this street.)

OTHER CELEBRITIES WHO LIVE IN
BEVERLY HILLS: Mary Hart, Michael Caine,
Danny DeVito and Rhea Perlman, Kirk Douglas,
Shelley Winters, Priscilla Presley, Don Rickles,
Dinah Shore, Abigail van Buren, Maria Conchita
Alonso, Frances Bergen, Glenn Ford, Raquel
Welch, Tony Bennett, Ella Fitzgerald, Janet Leigh,
Shirley Jones and Marty Ingels, Robert Loggia,
Shari Lewis, Rod McKuen, Matthew Modine,
Catherine Oxenberg, Anthony Quinn, Jesse White,
Betsy Bloomingdale, Phil Collins, and Ringo
Starr. Neil Diamond, Casey Kasem, George C.
Scott, and Sidney Sheldon live in Holmby Hills. In
1954 Joe DiMaggio and Marilyn Monroe lived for
five months at 508 N. Palm Drive, one street east
of Maple Drive. It is often referred to as their
"Honeymoon Home" and still attracts tourists.

77. RODEO DRIVE AND NEARBY BEVERLY HILLS SHOPPING DISTRICT

As one storeowner put it: "You'll see more Rolls
Royces (on Rodeo Drive) in ten minutes than you'll see
in Cleveland, Ohio, all year."

If you would like to tour this ultrachic shopping
district, contact the Beverly Hills Visitors' Bureau and
ask for their guide to the stores and their publication,
"A Guide to Beverly Hills," which includes a walking
tour. The Visitors' Bureau (310-271-8174; 800-345-
2210) is very helpful and offers a variety of services,
including an Ambassadear program which offers

multilingual docents who will host parties, take you on shopping tours, and treat you like a celebrity. For those who wish to spend some time in the shopping district, there are a number of notable restaurants in the Beverly Hills shopping district which attract a celebrity clientele, including one of Nancy Reagan's favorites, the Bistro Garden, 176 N. Canon Drive, (310) 550-3900; the Carnegie Deli, 300 N. Beverly Drive, (310) 275-DELI; Nate 'n' Al's Delicatessen, 414 N. Beverly Drive, (310) 274-0101. The Maple Drive Restaurant, which also attracts entertainment notables, is located just south of Wilshire Boulevard at 345 N. Maple Drive. For reservations call (310) 274-9800.

The Regent Beverly Wilshire Hotel.

78. REGENT BEVERLY WILSHIRE HOTEL, 9500
Wilshire Boulevard, (310) 275-5200, (800) 427-4354

Richard Gere and Julia Roberts stayed in the penthouse suite in *Pretty Woman.* (Although the outside of the hotel was used, the interior scenes were actually shot on a Disney sound stage.) Warren Beatty reportedly lived in the penthouse for over a decade.

OFF THE MAP are two sites in Beverly Hills that may be of interest to plastic surgery buffs. At the corner of Olympic Boulevard and LeDoux Road (one block west of La Cienega Boulevard) is the intersection where Zsa Zsa Gabor was stopped by a policeman in her Rolls-Royce in 1989. Zsa Zsa slapped the poor cop, resulting in worldwide publicity, a three-day prison sentence and one of the few motion picture offers she has had lately: a scene slapping a runaway police car in *Naked Gun 2 1/2.* The incident occurred around the corner from the Center for Motion Picture Studies at 333 S. La Cienega Boulevard, which houses the library for the Academy of Motion Picture Arts and Sciences, and where I conducted most of the research for this book. Also in Beverly Hills is Le Petit Ermitage at 9293 Burton Way. Profiled in *TV Guide, People* and other magazines, Le Petit is the luxury hotel where celebrities and socialites recover from cosmetic and reconstructive surgery.

☆ BRENTWOOD

1. UNIVERSITY SYNAGOGUE, 11960 Sunset Boulevard (between Westgate and Saltair)

Roseanne and Tom Arnold renewed their wedding vows here.

An aerial view of Roseanne and Tom Arnold's Brentwood home.

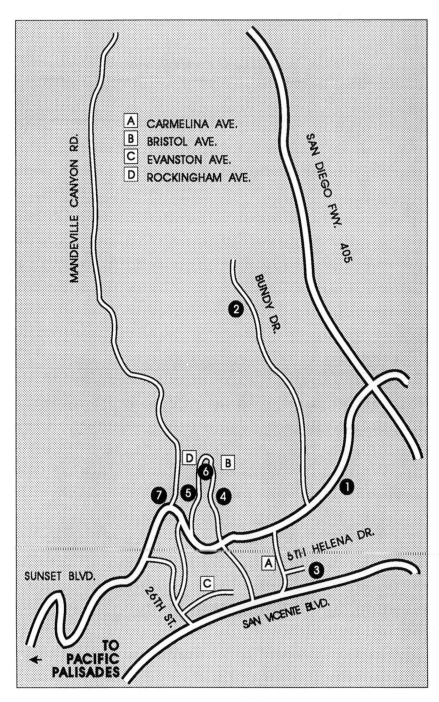

A CARMELINA AVE.
B BRISTOL AVE.
C EVANSTON AVE.
D ROCKINGHAM AVE.

MANDEVILLE CANYON RD.

SAN DIEGO FWY. 405

BUNDY DR.

5TH HELENA DR.

SUNSET BLVD.

26TH ST.

SAN VICENTE BLVD.

TO
PACIFIC
PALISADES

MAP 8 BRENTWOOD

2. *"SIX CRISES"* **HOME,** 901 N. Bundy Drive
   Richard Nixon leased this house after losing the 1960 presidential election. He wrote *Six Crises* here.

3. MARILYN MONROE HOME, 12305 Fifth Helena Drive (off Carmelina Street)
   Although some writers and conspiracy theorists allege that Monroe was murdered here because of her affairs with first John and then Robert Kennedy, Monroe died (at least according to the official autopsy report) of a drug overdose in her bedroom on August 4, 1962. She lived in this house alone with her dog Maf (short for Mafia), which she received as a present from Frank Sinatra.

Marilyn Monroe committed suicide (or was murdered) in this Brentwood home.

69

4. *"MOMMIE DEAREST"* HOUSE, 426 N. Bristol Avenue

In her book *Mommie Dearest*, Joan Crawford's daughter Christina told of being abused in this house while growing up.

5. SHIRLEY TEMPLE CHILDHOOD HOME, 209 N. Rockingham Avenue

Until 1951, Shirley lived at 209 N. Rockingham, while her parents lived next door at 227 N. Rockingham.

6. O.J. SIMPSON'S MANSION, 360 Rockingham Avenue

On June 17, 1994, a suicidal O.J. Simpson surrendered to police in the driveway of his estate after evading arrest earlier in the day for the murder of his ex-wife, Nicole Brown Simpson, and her friend, Ronald Goldman. The surrender climaxed an extraordinary day in which Simpson became a fugitive from justice and was chased by police over 60 miles of Southland freeways before returning home. The Hall of Fame football player turned sportscaster and actor was charged with killing Nicole and Goldman outside Nicole's condominium at 875 Bundy Avenue in Brentwood.

7. MANDEVILLE CANYON ROAD

This pretty canyon road, just north of Sunset, attracts an unusual number of celebrities. Karl Malden, Jill Eikenberry and Michael Tucker, Steven Seagal and Kelly LeBrock, and Julianne Phillips (formerly Springsteen), all own houses on the street, as do superproducers Fred Silverman, Allan Burns, and Ray Huggins. Former residents include Tom Selleck, Mark

Harmon and Pam Dawber. "Bonanza" star Lorne Greene lived at 2090 Mandeville Canyon Road for years. Dick Powell once lived on the 3100 block of Mandeville Canyon Road—and a location scout reports that the exterior of his house was used as the house in "Hart to Hart." It is not, however, visible from the street.

OTHER CELEBRITIES WHO OWN HOMES IN BRENTWOOD: Michelle Pfieffer, Veronica Hamel, Ken Olin and Patricia Wettig, Sally Struthers, Harrison Ford, Ron Koslow, Barbara DeAngelis, Dabney Cole-man, John Ritter, Luci Arnaz and Lawrence Luckinbill, Robert Culp, Pat Riley, Angela Lansbury, Joanna Kerns, Betty White, Mark Harmon and Pam Dawber, Hal Linden, Gary David Goldberg, Zubin Mehta, James Garner, Phyllis Diller, Meryl Streep, Rob Reiner, Blake Edwards, Martin Mull, Rod Stewart, Roseanne and Tom Arnold, Julie Newmar, Sally Field, James Belushi, Mimi Rogers, Randy Newman, Garry Shandling, Mickey Rourke, Norman Lloyd, Bea Arthur, George Carlin, Robert Wagner and Jill St. John, Anne Archer, Scott Valentine, Peter Bogdanovich, Jerry Rubin, and Pat Harrington.

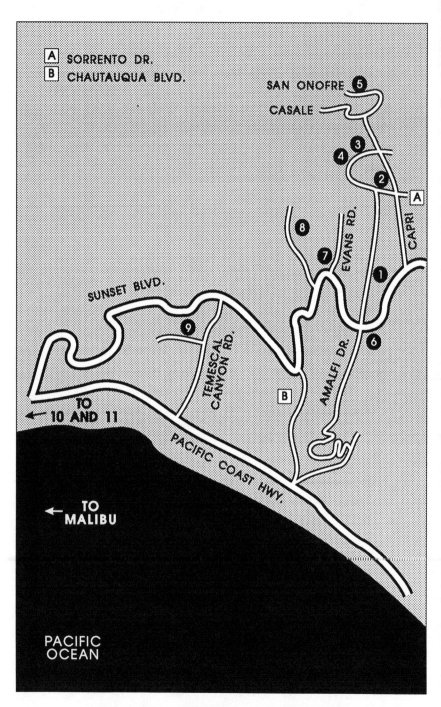

SAN ONOFRE ⑤
CASALE

③
④
②

⑧

⑦

EVANS RD.

CAPRI

A

①

⑥

SUNSET BLVD.

⑨

TEMESCAL CANYON RD.

AMALFI DR.

B

TO
← 10 AND 11

PACIFIC COAST HWY.

TO
← MALIBU

PACIFIC
OCEAN

MAP 9 PACIFIC PALISADES

☆ PACIFIC PALISADES

1. THE FIRST HOME OWNED BY RONALD AND NANCY REAGAN IN PACIFIC PALISADES, 1258 Amalfi Drive
The Reagans lived here from 1953 to 1956.

2. HOME OF TOM CRUISE AND NICOLE KIDMAN, 1525 Sorrento Drive
Cruise paid a reported $7 million for the house in 1990 and put the title in the name of his accountant in Century City. Foliage blocks the view of most of the house.

3. FORMER HOME OF SYLVESTER STALLONE, 1570 Amalfi Drive
When Stallone lived here, he constantly fought with his neighbors (including sports broadcaster Vin Scully) over the size of his trees and gates. The house sold in 1989 for $4 million.

4. HOME OWNED BY STEVEN SPIELBERG, 1515 Amalfi Drive
Five-and-a-half foot tall gates block the view of this extraordinary mansion that Spielberg lived in when he was married to Amy Irving. It was photographed in the May 1989 issue of *Architectural Digest*. Spielberg told the magazine: "The history of the house attracted me instinctively. It was important for me to know that David Selznick had lived there during the time he

produced *Gone With The Wind.*" Other previous owners include Douglas Fairbanks, Jr., Cary Grant and Barbara Hutton, and Bobby Vinton.

5. FORMER RONALD REAGAN HOUSE, 1669 San Onofre Drive

Ronald and Nancy Reagan bought this ranch house in November 1955 and lived here when he was elected president in 1980.

6. "DOOGIE HOWSER, M.D." HOUSE, 796 Amalfi Drive

Producer Steven Bochco, who lives on Amalfi, used a neighbor's house for exterior shots of the Howser residence.

7. EVANS ROAD, Pacific Palisades

Driving on this private road is prohibited by law, and if you get caught trespassing—and are convicted—you could be fined as much as $500 and thrown in jail for a year. Only residents and their guests can drive by Arnold Schwarzenegger and Maria Shriver's magnificent $3 million mansion, or the homes of his neighbors John Forsythe and Daniel J. Travanti. One of the homes on the street was used for exterior shots of Cybill Shepherd's home in "Moonlighting."

8. WILL ROGERS STATE HISTORIC PARK, 14253 Sunset Boulevard

Situated in this popular public park is the ranch house of humorist and silent screen star Will Rogers, who lived there from 1924 until his death in a plane crash in 1935. After his widow's death in 1944, the

The Pacific Palisades compound of Arnold Schwarzenegger and Maria Shriver.

grounds were presented to the State of California for use as a public park. The house contains artifacts and memorabilia pertaining to Will Rogers' career. (For house hours and information about the weekend celebrity polo matches, call 310-454-8212. There is a $5 parking fee.)

9. PACIFIC PALISADES HIGH SCHOOL, 15777 Bowdoin Street (west of Temescal Canyon Road and visible from Sunset Boulevard)

This is the high school immortalized by Michael Medved and David Wallechinsky in their bestseller *What Really Happened to the Class of '65?* Their book was a follow-up to a *Time* magazine cover story about American teenagers in the sixties which focused on Pali High's senior class of 1965. Pali alumni include Christie Brinkley, Jeff Bridges, Katey Sagal, and the Bangles' Susanna Hoffs.

(DIRECTIONS: To continue the Pacific Palisades tour and head toward Malibu, make a right turn at the intersection of Sunset and Pacific Coast Highway.)

10. SITE OF THELMA TODD'S ROADSIDE CAFE, 17575 Pacific Coast Highway (and 17531 Posetano Road, Todd's apartment above the cafe)

In the 1930s this building housed a popular celebrity hangout, Thelma Todd's Roadside Cafe, owned by Todd, a popular actress who appeared in 108 films, including *Horsefeathers* with the Marx Brothers. On December 16, 1935, the 29-year-old Todd was found dead in the garage of her apartment above the cafe. She was found slumped behind the wheel of her Packard;

there was blood on her mink coat and evening dress, the car, the garage floor, and on her head and face. Amazingly, the Los Angeles County coroner ruled her death an accidental suicide, leading to allegations that she may have been murdered, with the murder covered up by the police. Todd's ex-husband was connected with the mob, and rumors persisted that the mob wanted to use the cafe as a gambling den; Todd refused, and was killed for not going along with the plan.

11. J. PAUL GETTY ART MUSEUM, 17985 Pacific Coast Highway, (310) 458-2003

OTHER CELEBRITIES WHO LIVE IN PACIFIC PALISADES: Sydney Pollack, Goldie Hawn, Tommy Chong, Eddie Albert, Michael Keaton, Yakov Smirnoff, Dom DeLuise, Brian Wilson, Warren Littlefield, Rita Moreno, Tracy Ullman, Billy Crystal, Chevy Chase, Linda Hamilton, Walter Matthau, Steve Guttenberg, Marsha Mason, William Schallert, Diana Muldaur, Patrick McGoohan, Mark Grace, Harold Gould, Timothy Leary, Richard Dean Anderson, Bob Saget, Peter Graves, Kim Carnes, and John Travolta.

Thelma Todd's Sidewalk Cafe, circa 1935.

☆ MALIBU

"Malibu is the only place in the world where you can lie on the sand and look at the stars—or visa versa."
— Joan Rivers

1. CARBON BEACH

Carbon Beach is sometimes referred to as "Deal Beach" since so many entertainment industry executives do business from their summer or weekend beach homes here. "Dealers" include Disney Studios president Jeffrey Katzenberg; Columbia Television president Gary Lieberthel; and producers David Geffen, Aaron Spelling, Hal Ross, Jerry Bruckheimer, Alan Landsburg, and Robert Chartoff.

Carbon Beach also has its fair share of stars. Johnny Carson spent most of the 1980s at 22240 Pacific Coast Highway, which is where he spotted his fourth and most recent wife, Alex Mass, walking along the beach in front of his house. Carson later sold the house to John McEnroe for a reported $1.85 million and six tennis lessons. "Johnny was so serious about the lessons," Carson biographer Laurence Leamer wrote in *King of the Night,* "that the stipulation was included in the sales contract."

In 1991 Janet Jackson bought *Terminator* and *Aliens* producer Gail Ann Hurd's house down the street for $4.5 million.

Bruce Willis and Demi Moore have a home

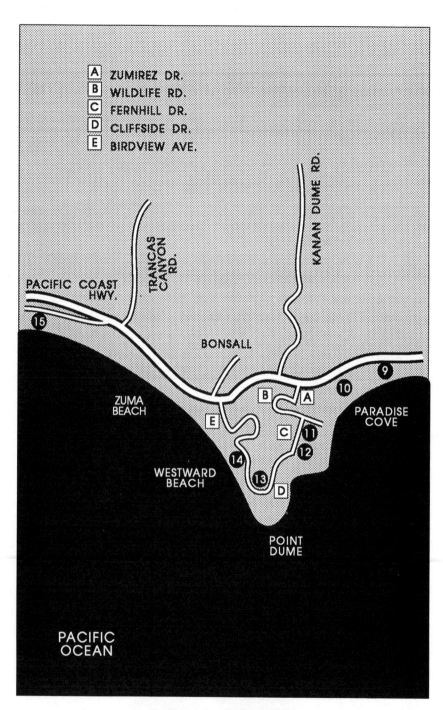

A ZUMIREZ DR.
B WILDLIFE RD.
C FERNHILL DR.
D CLIFFSIDE DR.
E BIRDVIEW AVE.

KANAN DUME RD.

TRANCAS CANYON RD.

PACIFIC COAST HWY.

BONSALL

ZUMA BEACH

PARADISE COVE

WESTWARD BEACH

POINT DUME

PACIFIC OCEAN

MAP 11   MALIBU

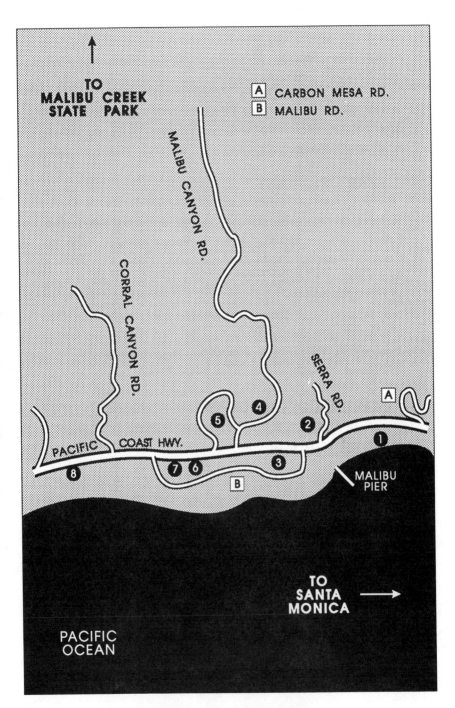

MAP 10 MALIBU

down the street. Others who own homes on the beach: Diana Ross, Henry Mancini, Lloyd Bridges, Brian Wilson, Dani Janssen (David's ex-wife), Flip Wilson, L.A. Kings owner Bruce McNall, record mogul Irving Azoff, Grammy producer Pierre Cosette, Jack Klugman, and Freddy DeMann, who is Michael Jackson's and Madonna's manager.

2. SERRA RETREAT

About seven miles north of Carbon Beach is Serra Retreat, a beautiful private community built around a Franciscan spiritual retreat—also called Serra Retreat—nestled in Malibu Canyon. Dick van Dyke, Mel Gibson, Charles Bronson, and George C. Scott live in this community.

The house seen in *The Doctor,* in which the characters played by William Hurt and Christine Lahti lived—and which was supposed to have been in San Francisco—is actually at 3701 Serra Road.

3. MALIBU COLONY (at 23554 Malibu Road)

Gates and armed security guards keep tourists out of this exclusive and snooty (according to some realtors) celebrity enclave. Colonists include Bruce Dern, Larry Hagman, Tom Hanks, Norman Jewison, Brian Keith, Burgess Meredith, John McEnroe and Tatum O'Neal (who moved here after selling Carson's Carbon Beach home), "Moonlighting" creator Glen Gordon Caron, and Sting.

(Note: Malibu Road was the setting of Aaron Spelling's miniseries "2000 Malibu Road," which revolved around four women who shared a beach house. The address was fictitious, but Malibu Road, just north of

A view of the homes in Malibu Colony.

Malibu Colony, also attracts many celebrities, most of whom own second homes there. Mel Brooks and Anne Bancroft, Tony Danza, Dom DeLuise, Shirley MacLaine, Dennis Weaver, Charles Bronson, Zubin Mehta, Bob Newhart, Don Rickles, Loretta Swit and Robert Altman all own houses on Malibu Road.)

4. HODGES CASTLE, 23800 Malibu Crest Drive
A real castle owned by a dentist. (You will see a few more when you take the Hollywoodland tour.) Patterned after a 13th-Century Scottish castle, the Hodges Castle is perched on a hillside north of Pacific Coast Highway, and can be seen from several directions, including from the gates of Malibu Colony.

5. PEPPERDINE UNIVERSITY, 24255 Pacific Coast Highway
Prestigious, picturesque and private, Pepperdine is a popular filming site. "Battle of the Network Stars" is filmed here.

6. FORMER HOME OF RICH LITTLE, 24734 Pacific Coast Highway
Little now resides in Las Vegas, and would like to sell his former home. He is asking $9,995,000.

7. HOME AT 24834 PACIFIC COAST HIGHWAY
In *Postcards From the Edge,* Meryl Streep shot at Dennis Quaid in this house, where Quaid's character was supposed to have lived.

8. GULLS WAY, 26800 Pacific Coast Highway
Brian Keith, playing Judge Milton C. Hardcastle, lived in this house in the 1983 to 1986 TV series

84

"Hardcastle and McCormick."

9. MALIBU GOLD COAST, 27700 to 27944 Pacific Coast Highway

You will not find the "Malibu Gold Coast" or any points north of Pepperdine on the Auto Club city maps. But if you continue north on Pacific Coast Highway, you will pass a stretch of land that talent agent Charles Stern dubbed "The Malibu Gold Coast"—which describes the beach-front strip of land that runs for a mile or so between his property on private Escondido Beach Road and Paradise Cove to the north. Celebrity residents include America's oldest teenager, Dick Clark (27700 Pacific Coast Highway), producer Jerry Weintraub, who has thrown parties for his friend, George Bush, at his home, "Blue Heaven," at 27740 Pacific Coast Highway; and a home at 27944 Pacific Coast Highway, where Blake Edwards and Julie Andrews lived for years. They sold it in 1992 for a reported $8.5 million.

10. PARADISE COVE

If you turn left at Paradise Cove Road, and head toward the Sand Castle Restaurant at 28128 Pacific Coast Highway (310) 457-9793, you will see where a number of popular TV shows have been filmed. In "The Rockford Files" James Garner parked his trailer in the parking lot adjacent to the restaurant; William Conrad's house in "Jake and the Fatman" was first house on the left of the restaurant. "Gidget" was filmed at this site. According to Art Fein's *LA Musical History Tour,* "the Beach Boys posed for their first album cover on this stretch of beach."

The former Unger Estate (left) and Johnny Carson's home (right).

(Note: The following three houses are located in an area known as Point Dume, south of Pacific Coast Highway. Los Angeles County filming records indicate that more permits are issued to film movies and other productions at beaches, homes, and other locations on Point Dume than anywhere else in the county.)

11. HOME OF JOHNNY CARSON, 6962 Wildlife Road

Carson purchased this spectacular retreat house, which is situated 200 feet over a cliff, for just under $8.9 million in 1985. According to his biographer Laurence Leamer, Carson also "bought the land across the street, and at a cost of several million dollars constructed one of the most remarkable private tennis court courts in the world. It was not so much a court as a mini-stadium, built recessed so that passers-by could not catch even a glimpse of Johnny playing each day."

12. THE FORMER UNGER ESTATE, 6970 Wildlife Road

In 1985 Madonna and Sean Penn were married at this palatial, $6.5-million clifftop home that was at that time owned by a friend of the Penn family, Dan Unger, who has been variously identified as a real estate developer and an attorney. In *Madonna Unauthorized,* Christopher Andersen described "the scene at the Unger home more closely resembled a war than a wedding. While armed security guards scanned the horizon with infrared binoculars looking for intruders—namely, members of the press—their blazer-clad brethren checked the credentials of each guest who passed through the ten-foot-high steel gates. Reporters dressed as waiters climbed over the walls, picked up silver trays, and began

serving sushi and Cristal champagne to the guests . . .
The publicity-loathing Penn, enraged at the presence of
the helicopters, ran down to the beach and scrawled
FUCK OFF in twenty-foot-high letters in the sand. For
nearly a half hour, he paced up and down the beach,
shaking his fists at the choppers and yelling profanities.
'He went,' in the words of one guest, 'completely nuts
. . . and emptied his gun at the helicopter.''

13. HOME OF CHER, 29149 Cliffside Drive
The Academy Award-winning actress and enter-
tainer, who was born Cheryl Sarkisian in 1946, divides
her time between this mansion and her other homes in
Manhattan and Aspen, Colorado.

14. WESTWARD BEACH
Music videos filmed here include Madonna's
"Cherish" and Vanessa Williams' "Dreamin." At the
end of the parking lot is the spot where Charlton Heston
finally fled from the apes in *Planet of the Apes.*

15. BROAD BEACH (six miles north of Paradise Cove)
It would probably be fair to say that more
celebrities own homes on this mile-and-a-half stretch of
land than in any other concentrated living area in the
world. Goldie Hawn, Carroll O'Connor, Georgia Rosen-
bloom, Jack Lemmon, Sylvester Stallone, Jon Bon Jovi,
Dinah Shore, James L. Brooks, Walter Matthau, Grant
Tinker, Frank Sinatra, Sid Sheinberg, Michael Ovitz,
Danny DeVito, Hugh Wilson, Dick Martin, Steve
Lawrence and Edie Gorme, Dustin Hoffman, Bernard
Brillstein, Steven Spielberg, Ralph Edwards, Robert
Redford, Neil Simon, Frank Wells, Tom Patchett, Walter

Hill, Thomas Pollock, Stephanie Beacham, Eddie van Halen and Valerie Bertenelli, and Sammy Hagar all own weekend or summer houses here. A few of these celebrities, including Brooks and Spielberg, own more than one house on the beach. Ted Danson, Chad McQueen, Mel Gibson, Emilio Estevez and Paula Abdul, Charlie Sheen, and Pat Riley have beach-front houses on the side streets off Broad Beach.

(Note: Tourists who wish to see celebrity houses up close can do so by walking through a public walkway next to 31346 Broad Beach. The fence is unlocked between sunrise and sunset. There are signs indicating where nonresidents can walk along the shoreline without trespassing.)

OTHER CELEBRITIES WHO OWN HOMES IN MALIBU: Pat Benatar, Gary Busey, Bob Dylan, Mick Fleetwood, Henry Gibson, Whoopi Goldberg, Burt Lancaster, John Larroquette, Linda Lavin, Craig T. Nelson, Olivia Newton-John, Nick Nolte, Sean Penn, Bronson Pinchot, Rod Steiger, Martin Sheen, Dean Stockwell, Danny Tartabull, and Cindy Williams.

Reminder: Do not approach or otherwise disturb the occupants of any of the homes in this book. Stay away from the occupants for your own safety!

Celebrity homes on Malibu's Broad Beach.

Ron Jenny's home on Pacific Coast Highway (not visible from the street) is a favorite of location scouts and has appeared in several movies, most notably *Terminator II*, where it served as the home of actor Joe Morton, who played Miles Dyson, in the movie. The windows you see here are the ones that Linda Hamilton shot out in an attempt to murder Morton and prevent him from inventing the system which results in a nuclear holocaust.

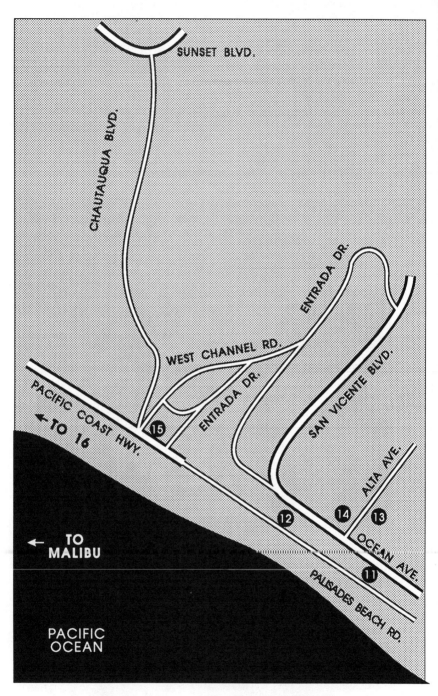

MAP 13   SANTA MONICA

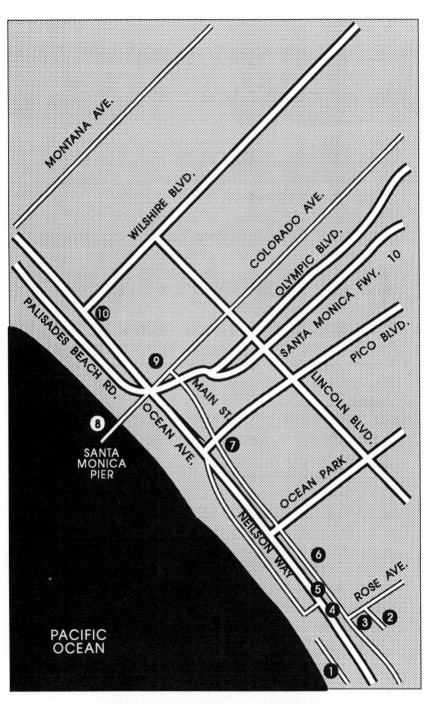

MAP 12 SANTA MONICA

☆ VENICE AND SANTA MONICA

1. OCEAN FRONT WALK (sometimes referred to as the Venice Boardwalk, Ocean Front Walk extends from Washington Boulevard in Marina del Rey to Marine Street in Santa Monica)

Most of the walk is along Venice Beach, which is famous for its street entertainers, bodybuilders, roller skaters, and the ubiqutious drug pushers, who can often be identified by pagers on their belts. On weekends the atmosphere is carnival-like. The beach here has appeared in countless movies (including *White Men Can't Jump*) and television shows. Fans of "Three's Company," starring John Ritter, Suzanne Somers and Joyce DeWitt, may recall the bicycle scenes at the beach in the opening credits.

2. GOLD'S GYM, 360 Hampton Drive, (310) 392-6004

For $15 (Gold's daily rates) you can pump iron alongside Arnold Schwarzenegger and other celebrities. Open 4:00 A.M. to midnight weekdays; 5:00 A.M. to midnight Saturdays and Sundays.

3. OFFICES AT 321 HAMPTON DRIVE

Once the Old Venice Gas Company, this converted warehouse now houses the production companies of Oliver Stone and Arnold Schwarzenegger. Visitors are not permitted, but occasionally you can see Arnold or Oliver at the Rose Café next door.

4. BALLERINA CLOWN, corner of Rose Avenue and Main Streets

"At the corner of Rose & Main," *Travel and Leisure* magazine notes, "is one of LA's newest landmarks, artist Jonathan Borofsky's monumental sculpture known variously as the Clown, the Dancer or 'that horrid thing.' It's a surreal combination of a clown's head, with a sad Emmett Kelly face, and the body of a tutu-clad ballerina: It's shocking, it's original, it offends the hell out of people. Whatever your opinion,

The Ballerina Clown in Venice.

95

the Ballerina Clown (its real name) serves as a great meeting place, since everyone knows where it is."

5. SCHATZI ON MAIN, 3110 Main Street, (310) 399-4800

Restaurant owned by Arnold Schwarzenegger and his wife, Maria Shriver.

6. STAR WARES ON MAIN, 2817 Main Street (between Ashland and Hill), (310) 399-0224

There are several boutiques in Los Angeles where you can buy clothes once worn by celebrities (usually women's evening wear and casual clothes). However, Star Wares is, at this time, the only store in town which actually identifies the celebrities who donated the items. In addition to personal clothing, this store has offered for sale a cape Elvis wore on tour ($50,000), Madonna's uniform in *A League of Their Own* ($6,000), the Terminator's steel skull in *Terminator II* ($4,500), the jacket Michael Jackson wore in a "Pepsi" commercial, Madonna's sweater from a *Who's That Girl?* video, an autographed Magic Johnson jersey, Richard Chamberlain's lab coat from "Dr. Kildare," loafers Bill Cosby wore on "The Cosby Show," RoboCop's right arm, "Star Trek: The Next Generation" uniforms, and the arm Arnold Schwarzenegger used in *Terminator II*. Catalogues are available on request.

7. SANTA MONICA CIVIC AUDITORIUM, 1855 Main Street (at Pico)

Site of the Academy Awards presentations from 1961 to 1968.

8. SANTA MONICA PIER, end of Colorado Avenue
(at Ocean Avenue)

Featured in countless television shows and movies,
including *Ruthless People; The Sting; They Shoot
Horses, Don't They?;* and *Funny Girl.* According to
Steven Gaines, author of *Heroes and Villains: The True
Story of the Beach Boys,* Brian Wilson once jumped off
the pier in a suicide attempt, but was rescued by his
brother Dennis.

The Santa Monica Pier.

9. SANTA MONICA PLACE (bounded by 4th and Colorado; 2nd and Broadway)

The mall scenes in *Terminator II* were filmed here, including the fight scenes between the two Terminators, which were filmed in the back hallways, and a scene in which Schwarzenegger was thrown through the window of the Oak Tree. The video arcade was built specially for the movie in an empty storefront. (The producers used the Northridge Mall at 9301 Tampa Avenue, Northridge, for the exterior shots). Also filmed here was the 1990 feature *Internal Affairs*. For this film, a police station was built on the roof of the parking lot where in one scene, Richard Gere beat up Andy Garcia in an elevator.

10. LAWRENCE WELK PLAZA, 100 Wilshire Boulevard (at Ocean Avenue)

The 22-story General Telephone Building, now part of the Lawrence Welk Plaza, served as the hospital front for the television series "Marcus Welby, M.D."

11. PETER LAWFORD'S BEACH HOUSE, 625 Palisades Beach Road

Once film mogul Louis B. Mayer's Santa Monica beach house, this mansion was later owned by actor Peter Lawford and his wife Pat, one of John F. Kennedy's sisters. In *Peter Lawford: The Man Who Kept The Secrets,* author James Spada wrote: "For the first two years of the Kennedy administration, Pat and Peter's beach house was essentially the Western White House. Officially, the President stayed at the Beverly Hilton Hotel, but he spent his days relaxing by his sister and brother-in-law's pool ... When he was at Peter

Lawford's house, he was there to relax and have a good time—and Peter saw to it that he did. Whenever Jack visited when Pat was away, Peter could be counted on to throw a party for him that included, in addition to Peter's show business friends, lovely young starlets, models—and hookers. After an evening of partying, Jack would choose one or two of the prettiest to return with them to his hotel suite. Some of the parties at Lawford's house—those peopled by a great many legendary beautiful women and a great many older married men—became legendary." Lawford's next-door neighbor told author Anthony Summers: "'it was nothing but La Dolce Vita over there. It was like a goddamn whorehouse.' And Jack Kennedy hustled his wife. He wanted her to go to Hawaii with him. 'It was the most disgusting thing I've ever seen.'"

12. "BEVERLY HILLS BEACH CLUB," 415 Palisades Beach Road

The site used as the beach club in the popular television series "Beverly Hills 90210" has an intriguing history. On the site once stood an 118-room, 55-bath mansion that newspaper magnate William Randolph Hearst built in 1928 for his mistress, actress Marion Davies, for a then unheard-of cost of $7 million. Producer Richard Zanuck, who grew up nearby, once remarked: "It made *Gone With the Wind's* Tara look like a guesthouse." The main house was torn down in 1955, but the servants' wings became part of an exclusive private beach club, the Sand and Sea Club. When the Sand and Sea closed in 1991, the state leased the property for filming—and "Beverly Hills 90210" used it as a focal point for its summer shows.

13. FORMER JANE FONDA HOUSE, 316 Alta Drive
Fonda lived here before she married Ted Turner in
1991. The home reportedly sold for close to its $2.7
million asking price.

14. PARK PLAZA CONDOMINIUMS, 515 Ocean
Avenue
Jane Wyman owns a condo here.

15. PATRICK'S ROADHOUSE, 106 Entrada Dr. (at
Pacific Coast Highway), (310) 459-4544 or 459-6506
Notorious celebrity hangout, and reportedly Arnold
Schwarzenegger's favorite restaurant.

**16. LIFEGUARD STATION, TEMESCAL CANYON
AND PACIFIC COAST HIGHWAY,** around 16000
Pacific Coast Highway
In TV's "Baywatch," David Hasselhoff oversees
the lifeguards at this lifeguard station, which is used for
both exterior and interior shots. Most of the beach
scenes are filmed by the station at Will Rogers State
Beach, although the show has also filmed at Santa
Monica State Beach, Venice Beach, Paradise Cove,
Zuma Beach, Marina del Rey and Long Beach.

CELEBRITIES WHO LIVE IN SANTA MONICA: Susanna Hoffs, Denise Crosby, Suzi Chaffee, Dana Delaney, Suzanne Somers, Jackson Browne, Paul Michael and Elizabeth Glaser, June Lockhart, Jeff Bridges, Ted Danson, Mel Brooks and Anne Bancroft, Michael Crichton, Roger Corman, Wes Craven, Amy Irving, Paula Poundstone, Joyce DeWitt, Kevin McCarthy, Randy Newman, Oliver Stone, Joe Regalbuto, Patti Davis, Michelle Pfeiffer, Wendy Wilson, Chynna Phillips, Sugar Ray Robinson, Tom Hayden, Debbie Allen, Glen Gordon Caron, Bonnie Bedelia, Dwayne Hickman, Blythe Danner, Lou Ferrigno, Jason Bateman, David Clennon, Tracy Nelson, Harold Ramis, Richard Dysart, Tony Goldwin, and Shelley Hack. Dennis Hopper, Matt Groening, and Barbara Del Geddis live near the beach in Venice.

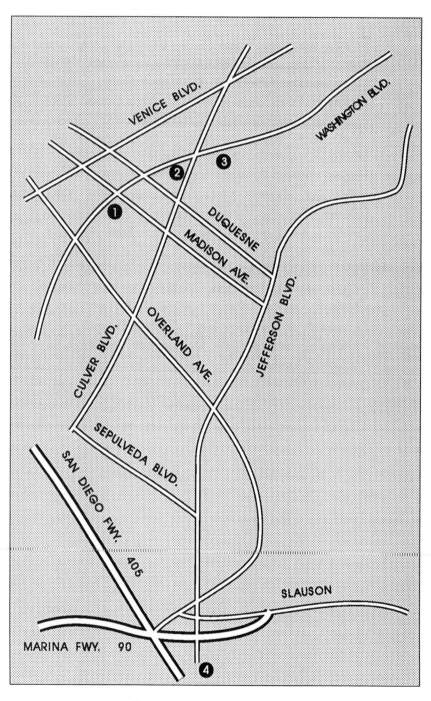

MAP 14 CULVER CITY

☆ CULVER CITY

1. SONY ENTERTAINMENT, 10202 W. Washington Boulevard

Located on the former MGM lot, Sony is the parent company of Columbia Pictures and Tri-Star Pictures, entertainment companies which film many of their features on the sound stages here. The studio does not offer a tour.

(Tourists looking for MGM can find its new offices at 2500 Broadway Ave. in Santa Monica.)

2. OLD CULVER CITY HOTEL, 9400 Culver Boulevard

In 1938 most of the Munchkins stayed in this triangular-shaped hotel during the filming of *The Wizard of Oz.*

3. THE CULVER STUDIOS, 9336 Washington Boulevard

Owned by Sony Pictures Entertainment and often rented out to other studios, The Culver Studios is the most interesting studio in Culver City to drive by. The main attraction is the neo-colonial white mansion seen in the opening credits of all the David O. Selznick movies, including *Gone With the Wind.* The burning of Atlanta and other scenes from the movie were filmed on the back lot along Ballona Creek, but the site is now an industrial tract. Selznick, who also produced *Rebecca, King Kong,* and the original *A Star is Born,* was one of many to own the studio. Others include movie pioneer Thomas Ince, Cecil B. DeMille, RKO-Pathe, Howard Hughes, Desilu, Laird International Studios and Grant Tinker. Interior shots for *E.T., City Slickers* and *A Few Good Men* were filmed here. Visitors are not allowed.

4. HILLSIDE CEMETERY, 6001 Centinela Avenue

When you drive on the San Diego Freeway (the 405), between the airport and the West L.A., you cannot miss the six-column marble shrine to Al Jolson, who appeared in *The Jazz Singer,* the first motion picture with synchronized sound. The memorial depicts him down on one knee, singing with his arms outstretched. Jack and Mary Livingstone Benny, Eddie Cantor, George A. Jessel, David Janssen, Allan Sherman, Percy Faith and Vic Morrow are also buried at Hillside.

(Holy Cross Cemetery, located at 5835 W. Slauson Avenue, is located nearby. Bing Crosby, Spike Jones, Mario Lanza, Bela Lugosi, Jimmy Durante, Sharon Tate, Ray Bolger, John Candy and Louella Parsons are buried there.)

☆ WESTWOOD AND CENTURY CITY

1. DEAD MAN'S CURVE, Sunset Boulevard (across from the UCLA football field)

Many people believe that "Dead Man's Curve," immortalized in song by Jan and Dean, referred to one of the curves on Mulholland Drive. Others believe it referred to a curve on Whittier Boulevard, by Buddy Hackett's house, where Jan Berry, one of the songwriters, was involved in a near-fatal car crash. (That accident actually happened after the song was released.) In *The L.A. Musical History Tour,* Art Fein reports that both Jan and Dean and co-writer Roger Christian agree "Dead Man's Curve" referred to a particularly curvy stretch of Sunset Boulevard across from the UCLA football field. Though most of Sunset Boulevard around UCLA and Beverly Hills remains curvy, Dead Man's Curve no longer exists. According to Fein, it was regraded after comedian Mel Blanc suffered a near-fatal crash there. (Note: The chase scenes from *Against All Odds* were filmed on Sunset between Veteran Avenue and Beverly Glen Boulevard.)

2. UCLA, 405 Hilgard Avenue

UCLA boasts one of the finest film schools in the country. Its dean, Gilbert Cates, is the executive producer of the Academy Awards and a director in his own right. UCLA alumni in the arts include the Jim Morrison, who, contrary to the impression left in Oliver Stone's *The Doors,* was actually graduated with honors;

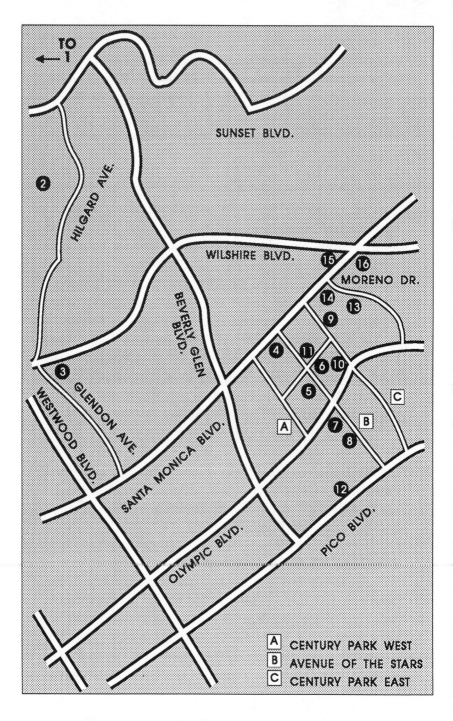

MAP 15 WESTWOOD & CENTURY CITY

Francis Ford Coppola; screenwriter Shane Black (*Lethal Weapon 1 and 2,* and *The Last Boy Scout*); Carol Burnett, Kareem Abdul-Jabbar, Michael Warren, Tim Robbins, Marilyn McCoo, Mike Medavoy, Michael Ovitz, conductor John Williams, Charles Burnett, and James Dean. Rob Reiner is one of UCLA's more famous dropouts.

UCLA is also a frequent location site. The 1985 feature *Gotcha!* was filmed extensively on campus. So were many scenes from Reiner's *The Sure Thing.* UCLA has also appeared in *The Big Fix, Final Analysis, Mr. Baseball,* and hundreds of commercials and television shows.

3. WESTWOOD VILLAGE MEMORIAL PARK AND MORTUARY, 1218 Glendon Avenue

The cemetery, which is a little difficult to find (the driveway entrance is tucked away between an office building at the southeast corner of Wilshire Boulevard and a parking structure), attracts tourists who wish to pay their respects to Marilyn Monroe. Near Marilyn's crypt, which is located in the Corridors of Memories, are the graves of two of the children from the *Poltergiest* movies (Dominique Dunne, who was strangled by her boyfriend; and Heather "They're here" O'Rourke, who died of a rare intestinal deformity at the age of 12); 1980 *Playboy* Playmate of the Year Dorothy Stratten, whose story was memorialized in the chilling *Star 80* starring Eric Roberts and Mariel Hemingway; Darryl F. Zanuck; historians Will and Ariel Durant; Natalie Wood; Donna Reed; Truman Capote; Buddy Rich; and Roy Orbison. Peter Lawford was buried here, but his last wife Patty removed Lawford's ashes when cemetary officials insisted Lawford's crypt be fully paid for. According to

James Spada, author of *Peter Lawford: The Man Who Kept the Secrets,* when Lawford was evicted from the cemetery, Patty made a deal with the *National Enquirer,* "giving the tabloid exclusive picture rights in exchange for the limousine to take her to Marina del Rey, and a boat which to scatter Peter's ashes in the Pacific . . . Newspapers around the country told the story of Peter Lawford's last great indignity—his eviction from his final resting place."

4. CENTURY CITY SHOPPING CENTER & MARKETPLACE, 10250 Santa Monica Boulevard, (310) 277-3898

Offers free parking for three hours. More and more movie premieres are held at the theaters here.

5. CENTURY PLAZA HOTEL AND TOWER, 2025 Avenue of the Stars

One of Los Angeles' premier hotels, the Century Plaza is a frequent site of celebrity fundraisers. In 1972 Marilyn McCoo and Billy Davis, Jr., of the Fifth Dimension, were married behind the hotel and flew up, up and away in a hot air balloon.

6. ABC ENTERTAINMENT CENTER, 2020 and 2040 Avenue of the Stars

The complex includes the Shubert Theater, movie theaters, offices, and restaurants.

7. FOX PLAZA, 2121 Avenue of the Stars

Located just yards from the back gate of 20th Century Fox, this is the building used as the site of the Nakatomi Corporation in *Die Hard.* Bruce Willis tried to rescue hostages taken in the 33rd and 34th floors of the

A view of Century City, including the Century Plaza Towers center), Fox Plaza, where *Die Hard* was filmed (right), and 20th Century Fox (bottom right).

109

building, which was chosen for its high-tech look. Ironically, the building, owned by Fox at the time of the filming, was later sold to a Japanese concern. Ronald Reagan has offices here.

8. J. W. MARRIOTT HOTEL AT CENTURY CITY, 2151 Avenue of the Stars (at Galaxy Way), (310) 277-2777; (800) 228-9290

In *Lethal Weapon 2* Mel Gibson and Danny Glover guarded Joe Pesci in the presidential suite of the J. W. Marriott, and their stuntmen jumped into the swimming pool. (The Marriott was also used for the pool jump scene in *Harley Davidson and the Marlboro Man.*) Also filmed here were the scenes in *Pacific Heights* in which Melanie Griffith, investigating Michael Keaton, tracked him to a room at the hotel. In *Point of No Return*, Bridget Fonda planted a bomb, which destroyed part of the hotel.

9. HOME OF ORION PICTURES, 1888 Century Park East

Orion, which produced *The Silence of the Lambs* and *Dances With Wolves,* was once considered a major Hollywood studio, but now primarily functions as a film distributor.

10. CENTURY PLAZA TOWERS, 2029 and 2049 Century Park East

These twin office towers served as the exteriors of Cybill Shepherd and Bruce Willis' Blue Moon Detective Agency in "Moonlighting," and Stephanie Zimbalist and Pierce Brosnan's Steele Investigations in "Remington Steele."

11. TRIPP'S RESTAURANT, (formerly Hy's) 10131 Constellation Boulevard, (310) 553-6000

According to the magazine *Location Update*, Tripp's was "the heavenly establishment in *Defending Your Life's* Judgment City where Albert Brooks and Meryl Streep were able to eat all they wanted without gaining weight. 'L.A. Law' also has a record of filming at Tripp's."

12. TWENTIETH CENTURY FOX, 10201 W. Pico Boulevard

Fox does not offer public tours, and the only way to catch a glimpse of its back lot is to get tickets for one of the shows filming on the lot from one of the audience service companies. From the main entrance on Pico Boulevard, you can see part of the set built for *Hello Dolly!* in the late 1960s. The studio has been located here since 1928.

13. BEVERLY HILLS HIGH SCHOOL, 241 S. Moreno Drive, Beverly Hills

Tourists drive past Beverly Hills High School thinking they will see fictional West Beverly High from television's "Beverly Hills 90210." The producers used Torrance High School in that Los Angeles suburb, where filming costs are lower. Beverly Hills High School is of interest as one of the best high schools in country. Its celebrity graduates include Shaun and Patrick Cassidy, Richard Chamberlain, Nicolas Cage, Barry Diller, Richard Dreyfuss, Nora Ephron, Rhonda Fleming, Bonnie Franklin, Joel Grey, Rob Reiner, Marlo Thomas, Burt Ward, and Desi Arnaz, Jr. *It's a Wonderful Life* was filmed on campus and there is a scene in the movie in which Jimmy Stewart and Donna Reed fell into the swimming pool there.

14. JIMMY'S RESTAURANT, 201 Moreno Drive, (213) 879-2394

A power restaurant that attracts more politicians that entertainers.

15. BEVERLY HILTON, 9876 Wilshire Boulevard, (310) 274-7777

The first Grammy Awards ceremonies were held at this hotel, owned by entertainer/businessman Merv Griffin. After losing the California gubernatorial race in 1962, Richard Nixon made his famous "you-won't-have-Nixon-to-kick-around-anymore" speech here.

16. HEADQUARTERS OF CREATIVE ARTISTS AGENCY (CAA), 9830 Wilshire Boulevard

Creative Artists Agency, which is headed by Michael Ovitz, is generally regarded to be the most powerful talent-management agency in Hollywood. Its three-story headquarters was designed by the internationally renowned architect I. M. Pei.

CELEBRITIES WHO OWN HOMES IN WESTWOOD AND CENTURY CITY: Placido Domingo, Brigitte Nielsen, Charles Durning, and Jim Nabors all live in high-rises on Wilshire Boulevard, while Carol Burnett, Rhonda Fleming, Don Adams, and Lana Turner own condos in Century City. "Hard Copy," quoting pop star Michael Jackson's former maid, identified the Westford condominium at 10750 Wilshire Boulevard as "The Hideaway" where Jackson took his "special friends."

☆ THE SUNSET STRIP

NOTE TO READERS: This is mostly a walking tour of what is often called Hollywood's playground: the Sunset Strip. This tour also includes a few homes in the hills north of the Strip which are best reachable by car. Most of the sites in this tour are within the city limits of West Hollywood (the dividing line between Los Angeles and West Hollywood is Sunset Boulevard; anything north of the Boulevard or east of The Chateau Marmont is within Los Angeles city limits). Sites south of Sunset Boulevard are included in the West Hollywood section. Those who walk the Strip should keep in mind that a few sites listed in the West Hollywood section, including the apartment where Sal Mineo was stabbed to death, and the apartment where Judith Campbell Exner lived when she had her affair with JFK, are within one or two blocks of Sunset Boulevard.

1. FORMER SITE OF SCHWAB'S PHARMACY, 8024 Sunset Boulevard (southeast corner of Crescent Heights)

Schwab's was the most famous drugstore in America, partly because its owner, pharmacist Leon Schwab, kept claiming that Lana Turner was "discovered" sitting on a stool at the soda fountain in his store. Turner herself has said on several occasions that there is no truth to the story, and it appears the tale was concocted by Schwab's publicist to lure customers to the store. There is, at least, truth to the story that in its

113

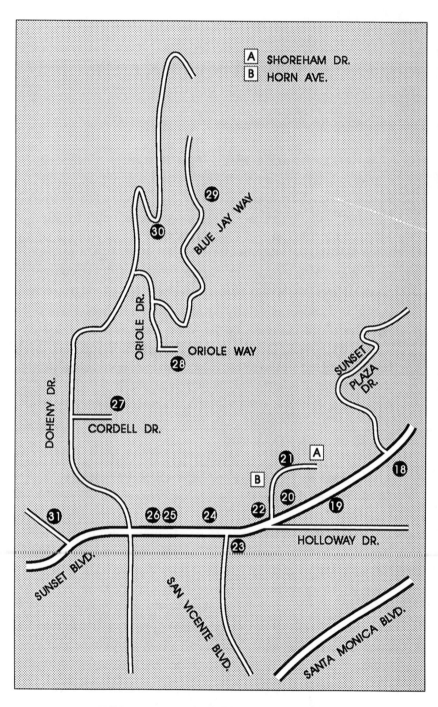

MAP 17 THE SUNSET STRIP

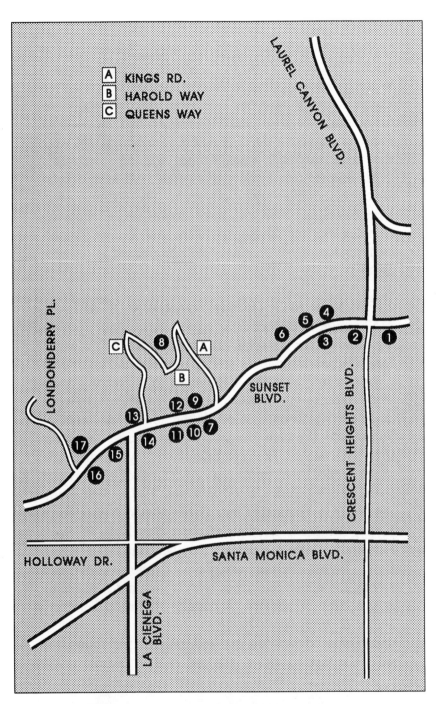

LAUREL CANYON BLVD.

LONDONDERRY PL.

CRESCENT HEIGHTS BLVD.

SUNSET BLVD.

LA CIENEGA BLVD.

HOLLOWAY DR.

SANTA MONICA BLVD.

MAP 16   THE SUNSET STRIP

heyday Schwab's was a popular hangout for writers and actors looking for work. In the movie *Sunset Boulevard,* William Holden called it "a combination office, coffee klatch and waiting room." Schwab filled prescriptions for studio executives and claimed he told them about some of the young budding actors who he thought were star material. While Lana Turner was not discovered there, one regular, F. Scott Fitzgerald, did have a heart attack there while buying cigarettes. The pharmacy was torn down in 1988 to make room for a shopping complex, but the developers claim that a more glamorized version of the pharmacy will be opened in the new complex.

2. FORMER SITE OF THE GARDEN OF ALLAH,
8152 Sunset Boulevard

Remember the song "Big Yellow Taxi," in which Joni Mitchell sang about paving paradise and putting up a parking lot? That was a reference to the tearing down of the the Garden of Allah, another famous Hollywood landmark which once stood on the southwest corner of Sunset and Crescent Heights, directly across the street from Schwab's. The apartment/hotel was what one writer called the unofficial epicenter of Hollywood social activity during the 1930s and 1940s, with Frank Sinatra, Ava Gardner, Clark Gable, David Niven, Errol Flynn, the Marx Brothers, Robert Benchley, F. Scott Fitzgerald, Gilbert Roland, Tallulah Bankhead, Clara Bow, Ernest Hemingway, and Leopold Stokowski among the major celebrities who were Garden residents at one time or another. According to Bruce Torrence, author of *Hollywood: The First 100 Years*: "It was not uncommon to see tourists and movie fans lining the sidewalk just to get a glimpse of their favorite star."

116

Torrence called the Garden's inhabitants "a fast-living, hard-drinking, high-rolling lot who burned out fast and took the Garden with them." In 1950 the Garden was sold to Lytton Savings and Loan, which tore it down and built its home office at the site. The site is now a minimall and a branch of Great Western Bank.

3. "ROCKY AND BULLWINKLE" STATUE, 8218 Sunset Boulevard

This converted house, once owned by Fess Parker and now occupied by an advertising company, was for years the offices of Jay Ward Productions, the animation company that created "Rocky and Bullwinkle." A 15-foot-tall plaster statue of the famous moose and squirrel still stands in front of the building, as does a small courtyard which bears signatures of June Foray (the voices of both Rocky and Natasha) and, strangely enough, the elbowprints of the cartoon's writers. Rocky and Bullwinkle saluted a once-existing billboard for a Las Vegas hotel in the 1960s, which featured a showgirl in a bathing suit. Whenever the showgirl got a new bathing suit, Bullwinkle got a new one with colors to match.

4. CHATEAU MARMONT, 8221 Sunset Boulevard, (213) 656-1010

When celebrities visiting Los Angeles want to be seen, they often go to the Beverly Hills Hotel. When they wish to keep out of the limelight they often stay at the Marmont, which one-time owner Raymond L. Sarlot called "Hollywood's authenthic Grand Hotel." In his book *Life at the Marmont,* co-authored with Fred E. Basten, Sarlot noted that the Marmont remains "one of [Hollywood's] best kept secrets, much to the joy of its

117

The coroner's van and the media circus outside the Chateau
Marmont on the day John Belushi died of a drug overdose.

118

celebrated clientele. Not too many years ago a *Newsday* journalist cornered Jill Clayburgh sipping coffee at Corrine's Corner. Following the usual career questions, she was asked to comment about her stay at the Marmont. 'Oh, don't mention the hotel,' she said, crinkling her face. 'Then all the tourists will come.' A moment later, Clayburg was on her way, but not before leaving the journalist with a final thought. 'If you must say something about this place, say it's terrible. *Please* say it's terrible.''' The fact that tourists have not discovered the hotel yet is one of the reasons why stars like Marilyn Monroe, Warren Beatty, Dustin Hoffman, John Lennon and Yoko Ono, Ringo Starr, Bob Dylan, Mick Jagger, Jim Morrison, Roman Polanski, Greta Garbo, and Helmut Newton have all stayed for extended periods. One former guest, John Belushi, did attract crowds when he died of a drug overdose on March 4, 1982, in Bungalow 3. In the movie *The Doors,* Van Kilmer, playing Jim Morrison, was seen trying to leap out of a sixth-floor penthouse.

5. THE ROXBURY, 8225 Sunset Boulevard, (213) 656-1750

The Los Angeles Times called The Roxbury ''L.A.'s hottest nightclub of the moment and a favorite of young Hollywood. On any given night, the crowd will probably contain familiar faces from MTV or 'Arsenio,' but they'll be upstairs in the rarefied air of the VIP room with Sly Stallone and Prince and Gerardo and a lot of other one-name stars. Dress to kill and you'll get in, but forget about the VIP room unless you're on The List.''

6. THE SOURCE, 8301 Sunset Boulevard (at Sweetzer), (213) 656-6388

Natural foods restaurant where Diane Keaton dumped Woody Allen in *Annie Hall*.

7. ST. JAMES CLUB, 8358 Sunset Boulevard, (213) 654-7100

Joan Collins, Sharon Stone, George Hamilton, Quincy Jones, Victoria Principal, David Bowie, Liz Taylor, Michael Caine, Liza Minnelli, Aaron Spelling,

The St. James Club on the Sunset Strip.

Jill St. John, and Richard Lewis, are among the many celebrities who belong to this exclusive club. Although it is a private club, the St. James does allow nonmembers considering membership to frequent the restaurant or stay overnight at the hotel for an $8.00 temporary membership fee above regular costs.

The building itself, an intriguing 13-story Art Deco tower emblazoned with mythological creatures, zeppelins, airplanes, and Adam and Eve, was once the Sunset Towers, the home to Hollywood stars such as John Wayne, Howard Hughes, Clark Gable, Errol Flynn, and Marilyn Monroe, Howard Hughes, Roger Moore, and the Gabor sisters. One resident, Bugsy Siegel, was reportedly asked to leave after he was arrested for placing bets at the hotel.

The club is occasionally used as a film location and has served as the outside of the Voltaire Restaurant in *Pretty Woman,* actor Stuart Margolin's apartment in *Guilty by Suspicion*, and Richard Crenna's apartment in the short-lived TV series "Pros and Cons." Tim Robbins was pitched a story idea at the St. James poolside in *The Player.*

8. LIBERACE HOME, 8433 Harold Way (between Kings and Queens Road)

Liberace lived in this 28-room mansion from 1961 to 1979. He told his biographer Bob Thomas, author of *Liberace:* "I tried to turn this place into a museum. In one month we had seventeen thousand reservations. But the neighbors complained" about traffic from the tourists. Liberace's museum was instead built in Las Vegas.

9. HYATT ON SUNSET, 8401 Sunset Boulevard (at Kings Road), (213) 656-4101

In the 1960s and 1970s, when the hotel was the Continental Hyatt House, and a favorite of rock and rollers, the hotel was better known as "The Riot House." According to Art Fein's *LA Musical History Tour* book, "Led Zeppelin rented as many as six floors here for their carryings on. Their partying set a standard that has never been equalled, with orgies, motorcyces in the halls, and stories yet untold." Fein also reports that "The Rolling Stones movie *Cocksucker Blues* shows Keith Richards and Bobby Keyes throwing a television out a window of this hotel" and that the Doors' "Jim Morrison lived here until he was evicted by management for hanging out a window by his fingertips, dangling over the pavement." Little Richard lived here through much of the 1980s.

10. SUNSET STRIP TATTOO, 8418 Sunset Boulevard

This is the place where Cher, Keifer Sutherland, Julia Roberts, Charlie Sheen, Lenny Kravitz and Lisa Bonet have all decorated their bodies.

11. BUTTERFIELD'S, 8426 Sunset Boulevard, (213) 656-3055

This patio restaurant was built on the site of John Barrymore's former bungalow.

12. COMEDY STORE, 8433 Sunset Boulevard, (213) 656-6225

One of Los Angeles' premier comedy clubs, the Comedy Store has featured performances from every important comedian. The names of its headliners are vaunted on its outside walls. This was once the site of

Ciro's, one of Hollywood's most popular nightclubs during the 1940s and 1950s.

13. PLAZA DEL SOL, 8439 Sunset Boulevard

This Spanish Revival apartment building was designated a historic landmark because of its beauty, not because of its notorious history. During the 1930s, this was reportedly one of the sites of Lee Francis' "House of Francis," the classiest brothel on the Sunset Strip. The building now houses the offices of several production companies—the names of which most people would not recognize, and the brothels are now located in private homes above the Strip.

14. MONDRIAN HOTEL, 8440 Sunset Boulevard (at Queens Road), (213) 650-8999

The red, orange and gray cubes painted on the side of the building may please some and assault the aesthetic sense of others, but this is unquestionably a classy hotel often frequented by record business executives and singers. One guest, Robert Pilatus of the pop group Milli Vanilli, tried to commit suicide here by slashing his wrist and taking prescription pills before dangling from a ninth-floor hotel balcony, and had to be rescued by sheriff's deputies. Pilatus was reportedly despondent over the scandal in which he had been caught lip-syncing. According to the hotel's manager, members of Guns and Roses, Public Enemy, Gipsy Kings, and Poison, as well as actors in town for a few months' movie shootings have all stayed here. Michael J. Fox stayed in Room 1110 in the movie *Doc Hollywood.*

15. SITE OF "77 SUNSET STRIP," 8532 Sunset Boulevard

Although fans of the popular 1950s TV series would never recognize it today, the front door of the Tiffany Theater is where Efrem Zimbalist, Jr., and Roger Smith played private eye at the fictitious address "77 Sunset Strip." The restaurant next to their offices, Dino's Lodge—which was once owned by Dean Martin—is also gone. It has been replaced by an office building housing Casablanca Records. Fans of the show will remember Edd "Kookie" Byrnes, the Jason Priestly of his day, parking cars at Dino's Lodge.

16. PLAYBOY STUDIO WEST, 8560 Sunset Boulevard

Location of Playboy Studio West, where many of Playboy's famous centerfolds and photo layouts are shot. Sorry, guys, no tours.

17. APARTMENT AT 1326 LONDONDERRY VIEW (one block north of Sunset, off Londonderry Place)

Jane Wyman lived in apartment 5 here in the late 1930s, just three blocks from Ronald Reagan's house at 1128 Cory Avenue. After they married on January 26, 1940, Reagan moved in with her. However, the apartment proved to be too small after their first daughter, Maureen, was born, and the Reagans built a house at nearby 9137 Cordell Drive (covered later on the tour, page 127.)

18. SUNSET PLAZA

This is a two-block cluster of hip outdoor cafes, boutiques, hair salons, and other stores whose prices rival those of Rodeo Drive's. It is one of the best people-watching places in town.

(NOTE: Tourists often ask how to get to the top of the mountain above the Sunset Strip to get some of the most commanding views of the Strip and the city below. It is possible to get there by taking a side trip up Sunset Plaza Drive. Just follow it continuously for about fifteen minutes, as Sunset Plaza Drive becomes Appian Way at the crest of the mountain. Then make a right onto Stanley Hills, and another right on Lookout Mountain, which dead-ends at Laurel Canyon Boulevard. Turn right on Laurel Canyon if you want to return to the Strip. This is not my favorite tour through the Hollywood Hills—the homes are not as unique or as impressive as they are elsewhere in the Hills—but the trip is worth trying once.)

19. LE DÔME RESTAURANT, 8720 Sunset Boulevard, (310) 659-6919

People magazine calls "the mammoth circular bar at Le Dôme one of L.A.'s best meet-and-mate spots. Here Sylvester Stallone often wooed Brigitte Nielsen, Rod Stewart met Rachel Hunter, and Don Johnson and Melanie Griffith rekindled romance." Author Jackie Collins calls Le Dôme "definitely THE place to have that power lunch."

20. SPAGO, 1114 Horn Avenue, (310) 652-4025

The most famous restaurant in Los Angeles and the place where the biggest stars party on Academy Awards Night.

21. SHOREHAM TOWERS, 8787 Shoreham Drive (at Horn)

David Lee Roth, Neil Sedaka, and Alexander Godunov are among the residents of this apartment/ condominium complex. Art Linkletter's daughter Diane, after taking LSD, jumped to her death from a sixth-floor apartment here in 1969.

22. TOWER RECORDS, 8801 Sunset Boulevard, (310) 657-7300

The store, which is often featured in national news stories about the record business, was held up by Jane Fonda and George Segal in the feature film *Fun With Dick and Jane.*

23. THE VIPER ROOM, 8852 Sunset Boulevard

On October 31, 1993, 23-year-old River Phoenix died of a drug overdose outside this nightclub owned by actor Johnny Depp.

24. THE WHISKY, 8901 Sunset Boulevard (at Clark Street)

This was the West Coast's first discotheque. "Go-go" dancing was born here.

25. THE ROXY, 9009 Sunset Boulevard, (310) 276-2222

The Roxy is one of Los Angeles' top music clubs and showcases for new talent. Although nearby restaurants claim otherwise, John Belushi had his last supper here at On The Rox, an exclusive private club above the Roxy.

26. RAINBOW GRILL, 9015 Sunset Boulevard, (310) 278-4232

Vincente Minnelli proposed to Judy Garland, and Marilyn Monroe met her future husband Joe DiMaggio on a blind date, when the Grill's predecessor, the Villa Nova Restaurant, was here.

27. HOUSE AT 9137 CORDELL DRIVE (north of Doheny Drive)

Ronald Reagan lived here with Jane Wyman from 1941 until their divorce in 1948. According to Anne Edwards' biography *Early Reagan,* he separated from Wyman several times during 1947 and 1948, and during two of those separations he moved into the Garden of Allah. After the house was sold, Reagan moved back to an apartment at 1326 Londonderry View. (After marrying Nancy Davis in 1952, Reagan moved into Nancy's apartment in Brentwood, and then they bought a house in Pacific Palisades.)

28. MADONNA'S FORMER HOME, 9045 Oriole Way

Madonna bought this gated 3-bedroom house for $3 million in 1989 from Allen Questron, the president and CEO of Neiman Marcus, and sold it during the real estate slump for $2 million in 1994.

30. BLUE JAY WAY (side street off Oriole Drive)

In his *LA Musical History Tour,* Art Fein reports that "George Harrison rented a house on this street in 1968, just before the Beatles recorded *Magical Mystery Tour.* Their publicist Derek Taylor had such difficulty finding the place in the fog one night that Harrison penned 'Blue Jay Way,' a dreamy paean to it, which emerged on that album. The street might still be hard to find, because residents report that the street sign is frequently stolen by Beatle(klepto)-maniacs.''

30. HOUSE AT 1654 DOHENY DRIVE
This three-story Spanish house is famous for two reasons. According to her memoir *Madame 90210,* Hollywood madam Alex Adams operated a brothel here for several years before her 1988 arrest. The house was later rented by Shannen Doherty, who, according to a lawsuit filed by her former landlord, left owing $14,000 in overdue rent.

31. SIERRA TOWERS, 9255 Doheny Drive
Jack Webb lived and died in this exclusive condominium. Actor Peter Lawford also lived here in the late 1960s and early 1970s, after he sold his beach house in Santa Monica. Lawford moved out of Sierra Towers after the 6.4 earthquake that shook Los Angeles on February 9, 1971, reportedly because he did not like the way the building swayed in the quake.

(Note: Tourists who wish to combine the Sunset Strip and Beverly Hills tours can do so by continuing west on Doheny. Hillcrest Drive—which is where the Beverly Hills tour in this book starts—is just two blocks west of Sierra Towers on Doheny, p. 19.)

CELEBRITIES WHO LIVE IN THE HOLLYWOOD HILLS ABOVE THE SUNSET STRIP: Bess Armstrong, Christina Applegate, Candice Bergen, Jim Brown, Rita Coolidge, Andrew Dice Clay, Richard Donner, Robert Downey, Jr., James Farentino, Larry Flynt, Jonathan Frakes, Teri Garr, Richard Gere, Robin Givens, Herbie Hancock, Katherine Helmond, Buck Henry, Sherman Hemsley, David Hockney, Tom Hulce, Jackee, Victoria Jackson, Martin Kove, Richard Lewis, Jon Lovitz, Virginia Madsen, Dinah Manoff, Ed Marinaro, Johnny Mathis, Marlee Matlin, Ricardo Montalban, Judd Nelson, Leslie Nielsen, Donna Pescow, Vincent Price, Richard Simmons, Cheryl Tiegs, Weird "Al" Yankovic, and Daphne Zuniga. Former residents include Harrison Ford, Carole King (who lived in a former Gypsy Rose Lee home now owned by actress Courtney Cox), and Ringo Starr. Buzz Aldren, Theodore Bikel, Carol Kane, Estelle Getty, Suzanne Pleshette, Amanda Donohoe, Jessica Hahn, and Jerry Seinfeld are among the many celebrities who live in luxury apartments or condominums just off the Strip.

TRAVEL TIP: Hollywood Heritage, an organization dedicated to preserving Hollywood's history, offers walking tours of Sunset Boulevard at noon on the second Sundays of each month. Walking tours of Hollywood Boulevard are also held on alternating Sundays. Both tours are well wortwhile. For further information, call (213) 874-4005.

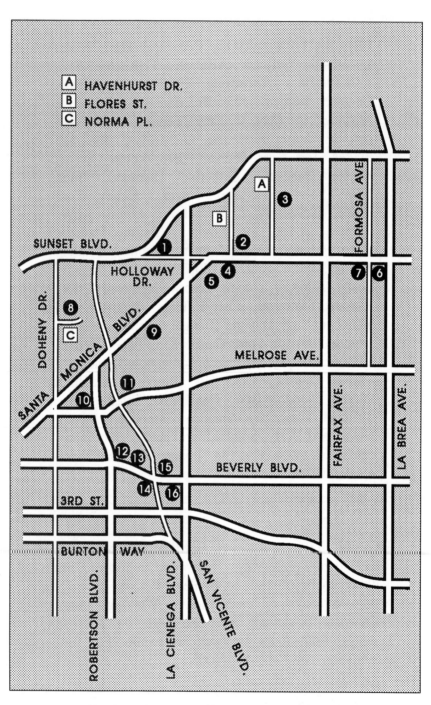

A HAVENHURST DR.
B FLORES ST.
C NORMA PL.

SUNSET BLVD.

HOLLOWAY DR.

FORMOSA AVE.

DOHENY DR.

SANTA MONICA BLVD.

MELROSE AVE.

FAIRFAX AVE.

LA BREA AVE.

BEVERLY BLVD.

3RD ST.

BURTON WAY

ROBERTSON BLVD.

LA CIENEGA BLVD.

SAN VICENTE BLVD.

MAP 18 WEST HOLLYWOOD

☆ WEST HOLLYWOOD

1. SITE OF SAL MINEO STABBING, 8563 Holloway Drive (one block south of Sunset Boulevard, between Alta Loma Road and Westmount Drive)

The 37-year-old actor, who is best known for his Academy Award-nominated performance in *Rebel Without a Cause,* was stabbed to death on February 12, 1976, in the carport of this apartment building owned by attorney Marvin Mitchelson. Mineo lived next door at 8565 Holloway Drive. Next door to that apartment, at 8573 Holloway, is another apartment that Marilyn Monroe shared with Shelley Winters in 1951.

2. FORMER APARTMENT OF JFK MISTRESS JUDITH CAMPBELL EXNER, 1200 N. Flores Street

Exner is the woman who had simultaneous affairs with President John F. Kennedy and mobster Sam Giancana during Kennedy's White House years. She also claims to have served as a courier between the two, carrying envelopes back and forth between them in 1960 and 1961. (Although she claims she never peeked inside, she believes the envelopes carried payoffs intended to influence in the 1960 election.) Frank Sinatra reportedly introduced Exner to JFK. In 1961 Exner lived here, in apartment 201. In her autobiography *My Story,* she claimed she was harrassed by FBI agents who learned of her affair with Kennedy, and in 1962 moved to another apartment at nearby 8401 Fountain Avenue.

3. COLONIAL HOUSE, 1416 N. Havenhurst Drive

Bette Davis, Clark Gable, Carole Lombard and her husband William Powell all lived in this French colonial apartment building. So did Sammy Glick, the protagonist in Budd Schulberg's classic novel of Hollywood, *"What Makes Sammy Run?"*

4. EMSER RUGS AND TILE, 8431 Santa Monica Boulevard (one block east of La Cienega Boulevard)

In the first *Lethal Weapon,* a suicidal Mel Gibson tried to talk a suicidal man out of jumping off the building. Gibson went nuts and they both ended up taking a plunge off the building into an air bag.

5. BARNEY'S BEANERY, 8447 Santa Monica Boulevard, (213) 654-2287

This old-time diner was once frequented by musicians like Janis Joplin and Jim Morrison. It is still considered a rock 'n' rollers' hangout.

6. WARNER HOLLYWOOD STUDIOS, 1041 Formosa Avenue

In the early 1920s, this was the Pickford-Fairbanks Studios, where Fairbanks made his classics *Robin Hood* and the *Thief of Bagdad.* Later it became Goldwyn Studios, and since 1980 it has been owned by Warner Bros. and used for the production of both motion pictures and television programs. Quinn Martin's shows, including "Barnaby Jones," "Cannon," "The Fugitive," were all filmed here, as were "Love Boat," "Dynasty," and the features *Basic Instinct, Oscar, Sibling Rivalry* and Eddie Murphy's *Distinguished Gentlemen.* The studio's Goldwyn Sound Facilities, which provided the postproduction sound for *Star Wars,*

Raiders of the Lost Ark and the *Rocky* pictures, is arguably the most prestigious sound department in the business. No tours; visitors are not allowed.

7. FORMOSA CAFE, 7156 Santa Monica Boulevard, (213) 850-9050

This famed Chinese/American restaurant once frequented by Marilyn Monroe, Humphrey Bogart and Clark Gable.

8. HOME AT 8983 NORMA PLACE

Humorist Dorothy Parker lived in this white stucco bungalow in the early 1960s; and it was here, on June 14, 1963, that she found her husband, Alan Campbell, dead. According to her biographer Leslie Frewin, in *The Late Mrs. Dorothy Parker,* a neighbor asked Parker: "'Dottie, tell me, dear. What can I do to help you?'" Parker answered: "'Get me a new husband.'" When the neighbor said how appalled she was by Parker's remark, Parker reportedly made her famous remark: "'Sorry. Then run down to the corner and get me a ham and cheese on rye and tell them to hold the mayo.'" (Incidentally, Norma Place is named after actress Norma Talmadge, who built a studio on the street. Dolly Parton owns a house on this street.)

9. THE SPORTS CONNECTION, 8612 Santa Monica Boulevard

This is the gymnasium where the John Travolta-Jamie Lee Curtis movie *Perfect* was filmed.

10. MORTON'S, 8764 Melrose Avenue, (310) 276-1253

Studio heads, superagents and their biggest stars

133

often do business over dinner here. *Spy* magazine's columnist Celia Brady always signs off each piece: "See you Monday nights at Morton's."

11. PACIFIC DESIGN CENTER, 8667 Melrose Avenue

Sometimes referred to as "The Blue Whale," the Design Center is the West Coast's largest resource for upscale residential and office furnishings. The building houses more than 200 showrooms to the trade. The building is open to the public; however, purchases must be made through design professionals.

12. CHASEN'S, 9039 Beverly Boulevard (at Doheny Drive), (310) 271-2168

Ronald Reagan's favorite restaurant. You are more likely to see "Old Hollywood" stars here rather than current celebrities.

13. HEADQUARTERS OF THE WRITERS GUILD WEST, 8955 Beverly Boulevard

14. CEDARS-SINAI MEDICAL CENTER, 8700 Beverly Boulevard (city of Los Angeles)

Hollywood's Grave Line Tour likes to point out that many celebrities (Danny Kaye, Sammy Davis, Jr., Lucille Ball, Peter Lawford, Jack Warner) died here. Of course, the reason so many stars die here is because it is one of finest hospitals in the country, and dying stars want the best. Mary Hart, Wolfgang Puck, Ronald and Nancy Reagan, Michael J. Fox, Tom Selleck, Jack Nicholson, and Warren Beatty and Annette Bening are among the dozens of other celebrities who have had children delivered here.

15. TAIL O' THE PUP, 329 N. San Vicente Boulevard

In the movie *Ruthless People,* Judge Reinhold made his ransom demands at this fast-food stand, which

The Tail o' the Pup hot dog stand.

is shaped like a giant hot dog in a bun. The Pup is considered to be one of Los Angeles' most famous architectural landmarks. It is so famous that when it moved to its present location in 1986, Robert Wagner,

135

Jay Leno and Billy Crystal hosted the reopening ceremonies.

16. BEVERLY CENTER, 8500 Beverly Boulevard at La Cienega Boulevard (city of Los Angeles)
The boring Woody Allen-Bette Midler feature *Scenes From a Mall* was supposed to have been set in the Beverly Center (although, with the exception of a few exterior scenes, most of the film was actually filmed at the Stamford Town Center in Stamford, Ct., and the Kaufman Astoria Studios in New York.) On the northwest side of the mall is the famous Hard Rock Cafe, which attracts a young rock crowd.

OTHER RESTAURANTS IN WEST HOLLYWOOD WHERE YOU HAVE A GOOD CHANCE OF SEEING SOMEONE FAMOUS:

● THE IVY
113 N. Robertson Boulevard, (310) 274-8303

● MADEO
8897 Beverly Boulevard, (310) 859-4903

● DAN TANA'S
9071 Santa Monica Boulevard, (310) 275-9444

● THE PALM
9001 Santa Monica Boulevard, (310) 550-8811

● HUGO'S
8401 Santa Monica Boulevard, (213) 654-3993

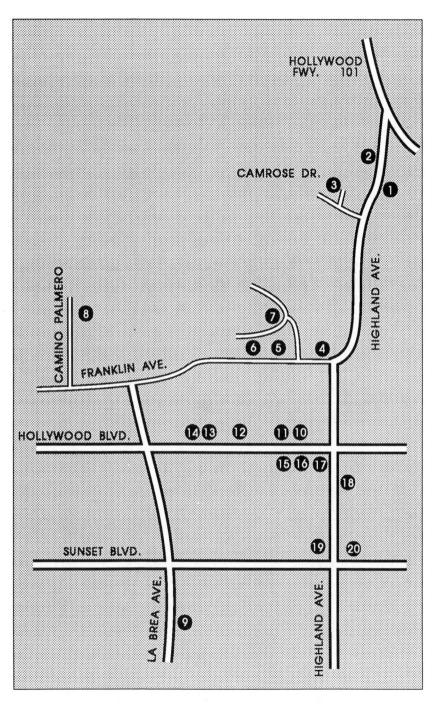

MAP 19 HOLLYWOOD

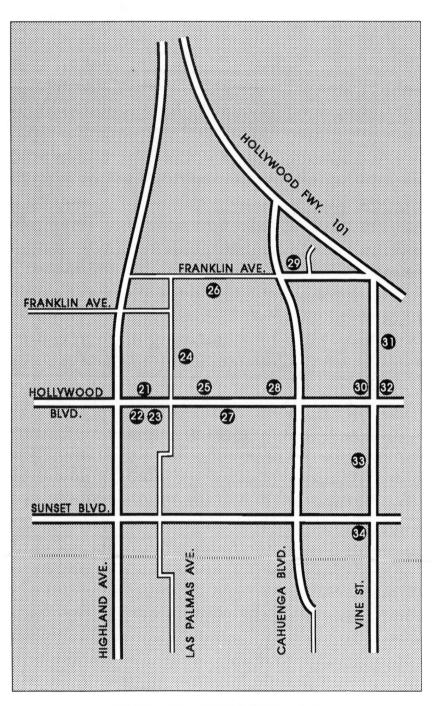

MAP 20 HOLLYWOOD

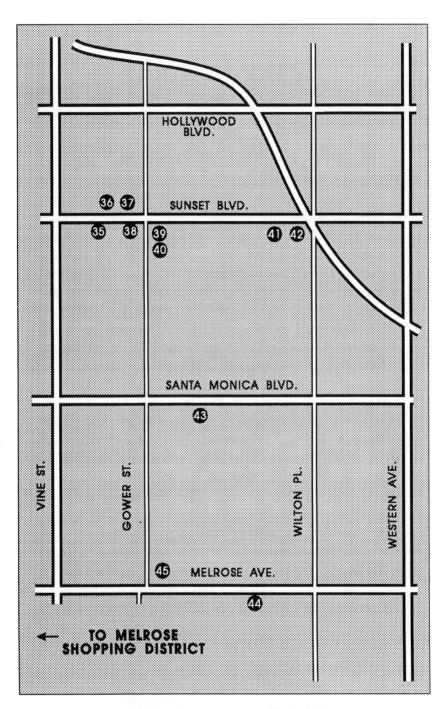

MAP 21 HOLLYWOOD

☆ HOLLYWOOD

1. HOLLYWOOD STUDIO MUSEUM, 2100 N. Highland Avenue

Dedicated to early Hollywood filmmaking, the Hollywood Studio Museum is located in the barn where Cecil B. DeMille directed *The Squaw Man,* the first feature-length film shot entirely in Hollywood. Some books give the erroneous impression that the barn is where the first movie ever filmed was made, but as museum director Kari Johnson points out, several filmmakers set up shop in Santa Monica and in downtown Los Angeles as early as 1906, eight years before the *The Squaw Man's* 1914 release. The movie's "real claim to fame," says Johnson, "is that it was the first nationally successful feature-length western." Its success also inspired other filmmakers to follow the lead of director DeMille and producer Jesse Lasky and set up shop in Hollywood. The barn, which was originally located a few miles east of its present site—at the intersection of Selma and Vine Streets—was subsequently moved to Paramount's back lot in 1926, where it was used as the railroad station in "Bonanza." The barn was later donated by Paramount Pictures and the Hollywood Chamber of Commerce to Hollywood Heritage, Inc., which operates the museum. Hours vary during the year; call (213) 874-2276 for information.

2. HOLLYWOOD BOWL, 2301 N. Highland Avenue

Since its opening in 1922, this world-famous

outdoor amphitheater has hosted performances by virtually every well-known musician. The Bowl Museum is open daily; call (213) 850-2058 for hours. There is no charge for admission.

3. HIGH TOWER (at the north end of Hightower Drive, west of Camrose Drive)

Fans of the 1991 suspense thriller *Dead Again* will immediately recognize this unusual-looking Italian

Hollywood's High Tower, where the climactic scene in *Dead Again* was played out.

tower. It was here—and in the studio apartment immediately to the right of it—that the climactic scene played out. The location was deliberately chosen (and even included in the original script) because the producers wanted to show that Emma Thompson, who lived in the apartment adjacent to High Tower, was literally cut off from outside help.

The five-story tower houses an elevator which services the houses and apartments built into the hillside. The elevator is inaccessible to the public, but the area offers some interesting photo possibilities.

Elliott Gould, playing detective Philip Marlowe, lived in the same apartment in the Robert Altman's *The Long Goodbye*.

4. FIRST UNITED METHODIST CHURCH OF HOLLYWOOD, 6817 Franklin Avenue

This is the church where Earthlings repelled invading Martians in the 1952 classic *War of the Worlds*. The gym inside is also often used for filming. The "Enchantment Under the Sea" dance in the first two *Back to the Future* movies were filmed here, and *Sister Act* was filmed in several rooms. Rehearsals for the feature film *Fame* and theatrical shows "Annie," "Cats," "Evita," and "Les Miserables," as well as auditons for Elton John, Rod Stewart, and Debbie Gibson videos, have also been held here.

5. MAGIC CASTLE, 7001 Franklin Avenue (corner of Orange Drive), (213) 851-3313

Once the home of actress Janet Gaynor, this Victorian mansion is now an exclusive private club for magicians. You have to be a member or an invited guest to get in.

142

6. HIGHLAND GARDENS (formerly the Landmark Hotel), 7047 Franklin Avenue (corner of Outpost Drive)
Janet Joplin died of a heroin overdose in this Hollywood hotel on October 4, 1970. She was 27.

7. YAMASHIRO RESTAURANT, 1999 N. Sycamore Avenue, (213) 466-5125
Yamashiro means "mountain palace" and that is what the restaurant is: an exact replica of a Japanese palace located in the Yamashiro mountains near Kyoto, Japan. Standing on a hillside some 250 feet above Hollywood Boulevard, and offering a panoramic view of the city, the restaurant was originally a private estate commissioned by two brothers who sold Oriental antiques. In 1914 hundreds of skilled craftspersons were brought from Japan to duplicate the Yamashiro mansion. The restaurant was later turned into a military school and at one point was converted into apartments where several celebrities, including Richard Pryor and Pernell Roberts, lived. In 1968 Yamashiro was transformed into a restaurant. It served as the officers' club in *Sayonara* starring Marlon Brando, and often doubles as "Japan" in commercials and television productions. Scenes from the 1992 feature *Man Trouble,* starring Jack Nicholson and Ellen Barkin, were also filmed here.

8. OZZIE AND HARRIET HOUSE, 1822 Camino Palmero
The Nelson family—Ozzie, Harriet, David and Ricky—lived here for over 25 years, and the outside of the house was used in their television show "The Adventures of Ozzie and Harriet." (In the early 1930s, movie mogul Sam Goldwyn lived next door at 1800 Camino Palmero.)

143

9. A & M RECORDS, 1416 N. La Brea Avenue (just south of Sunset)

A & M are the initials of the last names of the company's owners, Herb Alpert and Jerry Moss. They bought the studio in 1966, and have recorded artists such as Sting, Janet Jackson, Suzanne Vega, Amy Grant, Bryan Adams, and Rita Coolidge. The studio itself was initially built in 1919 by Charlie Chaplin, who made his classics *The Gold Rush, Modern Times, City Lights* and *The Great Dictator* here. In 1985, 45 top pop stars, including Michael Jackson, Bruce Springsteen, Stevie Wonder, Tina Turner, Cyndi Lauper, Lionel Ritchie, Diana Ross, recorded "We Are the World" here. (Note: Rock fans might be interested to know that just off the map—and half a mile west of A & M Records—at 7439 Sunset Boulevard, is the Sunset Grill, the eatery immortalized in Don Henley's song.)

10. MANN'S CHINESE THEATER, 6925 Hollywood Boulevard, (213) 464-8111

The Chinese Theater, which is undoubtedly the most famous theater in the world, opened in 1927 with the premiere of Cecil B. DeMille's *King of Kings*. Its forecourt includes the hand and footprints of almost 200 Hollywood legends—although some have left other trademarks, including Jimmy Durante's nose, Harpo Marx's harp, Sonja Henie's ice skates, Betty Grable's legs, Al Jolson's knee, and Donald Duck's webbed feet. The Mann Theater chain, which bought the theater from showman Sid Grauman, does not hold inscription ceremonies very often anymore; so you will not see the handprints of many of today's stars here (with the notable exceptions of Eddie Murphy, Harrison Ford,

144

A premiere at the world-famous Mann's Chinese Theater, circa 1964.

and all seven members of the original *Star Trek* cast). The 2,200-seat theater was also the home of the Academy Awards in the 1940s.

11. C. C. BROWN'S ICE CREAM, 7007 Hollywood Boulevard, (213) 464-9726

I thought that the store's claim that the hot fudge sundae was invented here was nothing more than typical shameless Hollywood hype—and this erstwhile investigative reporter thought he might be able to expose them,

145

particularly after checking with the International Ice Cream Association, which advised it had no information about the sundae's origins. Alas, there is no scoop here. Half a dozen phone calls got this author in touch with one-time owner Clifton Brown (now in his nineties) and he was able to explain how, for years, he experimented with different hot fudge formulas before perfecting the one now served on the sundaes in the store.

Tom Selleck's star on the Walk of Fame.

12. THE HOLLYWOOD WALK OF FAME (Starting Point)

Conceived by the Hollywood Chamber of Commerce in the late 1950s as a tribute to artists who have made significant contributions to the film, radio, television and recording industries, the Walk of Fame is often used by celebrities to plug their new movies, albums and concert tours. The "honor" costs $5,000 and is not always paid for by the stars. For example, Liza Minelli's fan club held bake sales to pay for her star. The selection process has generated some controversy. Blake Edwards, Dr. Joyce Brothers, and Suzanne Somers have all had requests for stars turned down. Some major stars—Dustin Hoffman, Clint Eastwood, Meryl Streep, George C. Scott, Jane Fonda, Sidney Poitier, Warren Beatty and Peter O'Toole, among others—have never bothered vying for the honor. The Walk, which now includes some 2,000 stars, and which extends from Hollywood Boulevard between Sycamore Avenue and Gower Street, and Vine Street between Sunset Boulevard and Yucca Street, is a popular tourist site. If you are in town, call the Hollywood Chamber of Commerce at (213) 469-8311 for a schedule of their forthcoming induction ceremonies.

13. FORMER SITE OF THE SCREEN ACTORS GUILD, 7065 Hollywood Boulevard

Until 1993, the building was the national headquarters for Hollywood's most famous labor union, representing some 76,000 performers. The new headquarters is at 5757 Wilshire Blvd., and is not open to the public.

14. STEPHEN J. CANNELL PRODUCTIONS, 7083 Hollywood Boulevard

Corporate headquarters of the production company that produced "Hunter," "21 Jump Street," "Riptide," "The A-Team," "Wiseguy," "Hardcastle and McCormick," "The Greatest American Hero" and "The Commish." Not open to the public.

15. HOLLYWOOD ROOSEVELT HOTEL, 7000 Hollywood Boulevard, (213) 466-7000.

The hotel welcomes and encourages visitors, especially those who eat in the hotel's Blossom Room, which was the site of the first Academy Awards ceremonies in 1929. That year the Awards were called the Merit Awards and Janet Gaynor and Emil Jannings were honored as best actor and actress, while *Wings* was named best feature. The hotel's nightclub, the Cinegrill, offers performances from well-known singers, and, along with Blossom Room and the hotel lobby, has been a frequent site for location filming. The strip tease show in *Beverly Hills Cop II* as well as a few of Michelle Pfeiffer's nightclub scenes in *The Fabulous Baker Boys* were filmed in the Cinegrill. The hotel's mezzanine includes a photographic exhibit tracing the history of Hollywood.

16. CITY OF LOS ANGELES FILM AND VIDEO PERMIT OFFICE, 6922 Hollywood Boulevard, Sixth Floor

A location scout once remarked to me: "It's funny how tourists, hoping to see how movies are made, always go to Universal Studios. If they really want to see how movies are made, they should go to the permit office [directly across the street from Mann's Chinese

Theater] and buy the shoot sheets. Then they can see for themselves how boring moviemaking is!''

Tourists who have never seen a movie being filmed may not find moviemaking as boring as jaded Angelinos do, and if they want to know what is filming around town, the city's film permit office has the answers. The office makes available to the general public a list—or shoot sheet—of all the motion pictures, television programs, commercials and videos being filmed that day outside the studios and within the city limits of Los Angeles. (The county of Los Angeles has its own permit office down the hall.) The shoot sheets, which cost $1.00 for the request and 10 cents per each photocopied page, provide the name of the production, the address where filming is taking place, and the time of day for which the permits are issued. Unfortunately, the shoot sheets do not tell whether the crews are filming indoors or outdoors (if crews are filming inside a house or building, chances are you will not see anything). To take full advantage of the shoot sheet one also has to be knowledgable about the different projects being filmed. The two Hollywood trade papers, *Daily Variety* and *The Hollywood Reporter,* print production charts which tell you who the director, crew members, and cast members of movies are; so if you buy the trades on the right days and cross-reference the production charts with the information on the shoot sheets you can increase your chances of going to a site where a major movie is being filmed. Many tourists, of course, do not have the time to do all this; so if you want to take full advantage of the shoot sheets, find a film buff or an independent tour guide who knows his or her way around the city.

17. EL CAPITÁN THEATER, 6838 Hollywood Boulevard (corner Orchid), (213) 467-7674

Recently restored, this Art Deco movie palace is one of Hollywood's architectural jewels. It is also the venue for Disney world premieres.

18. MAX FACTOR MUSEUM, 1666 N. Highland Avenue, (213) 463-6668

Max Factor was a Polish immigrant who, according to Hollywood promotional materials, "pioneered motion picture make-up and changed the face of the world. In 1929, he received a special Academy Award for developing the unique make-up used in panchromatic films." Factor reportedly created the first false eyelashes, eyebrow pencils, lip gloss, and face powder brushes. (The Art Deco building itself was dressed up for the movies and was used as the exterior of the jewelry store, Adriano's, robbed by Brigitte Nielsen in *Beverly Hills Cop II.*) The Museum is open Mondays through Saturdays from 10 a.m. to 4 p.m. and is closed on Sundays.

19. HOLLYWOOD HIGH SCHOOL, 1521 N. Highland Avenue

Until Hollywood declined in the mid-1960s, Hollywood High—and its drama department—served as sort of an unofficial actor's training ground for the studios. The school's alumni include Jason Robards, James Garner, Carol Burnett, Sally Kellerman, Stephanie Powers, Linda Evans, John Ritter, Jean Peters, Rick and David Nelson, Fay Wray, Mickey Rooney, Judy Garland, Nanette Fabray, Yvette Mimieux, Tuesday Weld, Swoozie Kurtz, Meredith Baxter Birney, and Barbara Hershey (although Charlene Tilton is the only television actor to have been graduated since 1970). In *Hollywood High: The History of America's Most Famous Public (High) School*, John Blumenthal writes that Hollywood High started going downhill in 1968 when the Los Angeles school board drastically shrank the Hollywood district boundaries: "As a result, upper-middle-class areas like Toluca Lake and Studio City, which had once sent their children to Hollywood High, were suddenly located in another district. 'That was the turning point,' observed Hollywood High English teacher Harry Major in the pages of *The News,* 'In one blow, we lost the cream of our students.'" By the mid-1970s, Blumenthal writes: "most recent alumni were clerk-typists, salespeople, factory workers, or stenographers."

20. FORMER SITE OF TOP HAT CAFE, 1500 N. Highland Avenue (northeast corner of Highland and Sunset)

It was at a malt shop once located at this site, not at Schwab's Pharmacy, that Lana Turner, then a student at Hollywood High, was "discovered" and turned into star. Turner told *Los Angeles Times* columnist Jack Smith that she cut a typing class and was in the shop when a she was approached by nightclub owner and *Hollywood Reporter* publisher Billy Wilkerson, who asked her: "How would you like to be in the movies?" Turner said her response was: "I don't know—I'll have to ask my mother."

21. GUINNESS WORLD OF RECORDS MUSEUM, 6764 Hollywood Boulevard, (213) 463-6433

22. HOLLYWOOD WAX MUSEUM, 6767 Hollywood Boulevard, (213) 462-8860

23. EGYPTIAN THEATER, 6712 Hollywood Boulevard (at Las Palmas Avenue), (213) 467-6167

Built by Sid Grauman in 1922, five years before the opening of the Chinese Theater, this was Hollywood's first movie palace. One of the more architecturally unusual buildings in Hollywood, the Egyptian was originally planned with a Spanish motif, but was redesigned with an Egyptian theme after King Tut's tomb was discovered.

24. "PRETTY WOMAN" HOTEL, 1738 N. Las Palmas Avenue (at Yucca Street)

In *Pretty Woman,* Julia Roberts lived—and was eventually rescued by Richard Gere—at the Las Palmas Hotel. (Note: Walking around this neighborhood at night or alone is not recommended.)

25. MUSSO AND FRANK GRILL, 6667 Hollywood Boulevard, (213) 467-7788 or (213) 467-5123

While Musso and Frank pride themselves for being the oldest extant restaurant in Hollywood, it is, more importantly, the only one on Hollywood Boulevard still frequented by entertainment industry types. The restaurant was seen in the opening credits of the short-lived television show about a young Hollywood agent, "The Fabulous Teddy Z."

26. MONTECITO APARTMENTS, 6650 Franklin Avenue (at Cherokee Avenue)

Ronald Reagan rented an apartment at the Montecito when he first moved to Hollywood. He lived here between 1937 and 1939, while working as a contract player for Warner Bros. Mickey Rooney, George C. Scott, Julie Harris, and Gene Hackman also lived in this former resident hotel, which is now an apartment building for senior citizens and handicapped people.

27. FREDERICK'S OF HOLLYWOOD LINGERIE MUSEUM, 6608 Hollywood Boulevard, (213) 466-8506

This Art Deco building (painted royal purple because purple is the color of royalty) is the flagship store of Frederick's and features a Celebrity Lingerie Hall of Fame which salutes stars of stage, screen and television who "glamorized" lingerie. The museum exhibits a Madonna bustier, a Judy Garland nightie, a Phyllis Diller training bra, and the first dress Milton Berle wore on television.

28. FUTURE SITE OF HOLLYWOOD ENTER-TAINMENT MUSEUM, 6433 Hollywood Boulevard (corner of Wilcox Avenue)

A $45 million museum dedicated to preserving and celebrating Hollywood filmmaking will open on this site in 1995. The museum will include state-of-the-art entertainment, exhibits, theaters, shops and restaurants. The space is now occupied by Pacific Theaters.

29. ALTO-NIDO APARTMENTS, 1851 N. Ivar Avenue (two blocks north of Hollywood Boulevard at Franklin)

In the classic feature film *Sunset Boulevard,* William Holden, playing unemployed screenwriter Joe Gillis, lived at the Alto-Nido Apartments.

30. CORNER OF HOLLYWOOD AND VINE

Although the legend of Hollywood and Vine lives on, the only things there today of even remotely passing interest are the Walk of Fame stars saluting Apollo XI

153

astronauts Neil Armstrong, Edward Aldrin, Jr., and Michael Collins. The astronauts were honored not for being the first men to journey to the moon, but because they appeared in an "outstanding television production"!

Beyond that, all the intersection has to offer is an office building, a fast-food pizzeria, a combination souvenir/grocery shop and a restaurant that appears to be closed. *Los Angeles Times* columnist Jack Smith opined that the corner "must be a letdown to [the millions of movie worshipers] who make the pilgrimage. It is the main corner of Anyplace, U.S.A."

Why then does Hollywood and Vine live on in the imaginations of movie fans? Well, back in the 1920s and 1930s, broadcasters used to announce that their programs originated from "Hollywood and Vine." At the time, most of the major studios—Paramount, Fox, Columbia, and Warner Bros., as well as NBC and other radio stations, many theaters and restaurants—were all located within a few blocks of the intersection.

"That's why Hollywood and Vine became famous," says Hollywood Studio Museum executive director Richard Adkins. "So many stars were working and spending their free time there."

31. CAPITOL RECORDS, 1750 N. Vine Street

The Capitol Tower, which was designed in 1954, is one of Hollywood's most identifiable landmarks. It is a circular office building resembling a stack of records with a needle on top (although the architect, Welton Becket, denied that he created the look intentionally). Capitol's artists over the years have included Frank Sinatra, Nat "King" Cole, the Beatles, the Beach Boys, Tina Turner, Donnie Osmond, the Doobie Brothers,

154

The Capitol Records Tower, one of Hollywood's most famous
landmarks.

Heart, Hammer, and the Steve Miller Band. The company's Gold Awards are on display in the lobby, but the company does not offer tours for the public.

32. PANTAGES THEATER, 6233 Hollywood Boulevard (just east of Vine), (213) 480-3232
Another extraordinary example of Art Deco architecture, the Pantages was the site of the Academy Awards in the 1950s.

33. TAV CELEBRITY THEATER, 1541 N. Vine Street
This is the theater where they film "The Love Connection." For tickets call (818) 506-0067.

34. CINERAMA DOME, 6360 Sunset Boulevard (corner of Ivar Avenue, one block west of Vine Street), (213) 466-3401
The Cinerama movie craze—in which movies were presented on three screens to give the moviegoer the illusion of being engaged in the action—died in the 1960s, but this geodesic-domed theater, built exclusively for those films, lives on as a conventional movie theater.

35. STAR SEARCH THEATER, 6230 Sunset Boulevard (just west of Gower Street)
In the 1950s the TV show "Queen For a Day" was filmed here. Jerry Lewis still films his muscular dystrophy telethon from this site.

36. HOLLYWOOD PALLADIUM, 6215 Sunset Boullevard, (213) 466-4311
Once the world's largest dance club, the Palladium has hosted Emmy, Grammy, and Golden Globe Awards.

"The Lawrence Welk Show" was also broadcast from here for years.

37. CHANNEL 2 KCBS, 6121 Sunset Boulevard (between El Centro Avenue and Gower Street)

The first motion picture studio in Hollywood—the Nestor Film Company—was originally located on this site. Nestor later merged with Universal Studios. In 1938 CBS built Columbia Square Complex, which houses Los Angeles' channel 2 and the CBS-owned radio station KNX.

38. GOWER GULCH, 6098 Sunset Boulevard (at Gower Street)

During the late teens and early 1920s, a number of independent studios—many of them fly-by-nights—operated in this stretch of Sunset Boulevard, and extras looking for work used to hang out in this area. Many came dressed in costume as cowboys and Indians, and someone named the area "Gower Gulch." To pay homage to that era the developers of the shopping center designed it to resemble a Western street.

39. COLUMBIA BAR AND GRILL, 1448 N. Gower Street, (213) 461-8800

The restaurant, which is located next to Sunset-Gower Studios, is the only restaurant in Hollywood where you are almost guaranteed to see someone recognizable. Here is a typical item from Army Archerd's column in *Daily Variety:* "Yesterday lunching at the Columbia Bar and Grill—Ronald Reagan and Arnold Schwarzenegger, A.C. Lyles and Frank Ryan. Seated next to those GOP'ers was Demo Norman Lear. And, in a back booth, Brandon Tartikoff and Frank Mancuso.'' The restaurant is such a hot spot that director Robert Altman filmed his scenes of a Hollywood power lunch in *The Player* here. Owners include actor Wayne Rogers, and prolific Hollywood producers Paul Witt, Tony Thomas and Susan Harris.

40. SUNSET-GOWER STUDIOS, 1438 N. Gower Street
        Once the home of Columbia Studios (now located in Culver City), Sunset-Gower is now a privately owned rental studio used mostly for television filming. When you drive by, you will see billboards with the names of the shows currently taping on the lot.
(Directions: The next two entries are both four blocks east on Sunset. To reach Hollywood Memorial Cemetery, go south on Gower Street and east on Santa Monica Boulevard.)

41. KTLA, 5858 Sunset Boulevard (between Bronson and Van Ness)
        This neo-colonial mansion was the original home of Warner Bros. and the site of the 1927 filming of *The Jazz Singer,* the first feature film which featured synchronized dialogue. When Warner moved its main headquarters to Burbank in 1929, this facility was used to produce "Bugs Bunny," "Porky Pig," and other Warner animated cartoons. Today the building houses Gene Autry's independent television station KTLA (Los Angeles' channel 5) and radio station KMPC. KTLA does not offer a tour.

158

42. FOX TELEVISION CENTER, 5746 Sunset Boulevard

This is the home of KTTV (channel 11 in Los Angeles). Some of the offices of Fox Broadcasting Company—which are also located on the 20th Century Fox lot (p. 111)—are located here. For information about obtaining tickets to tapings of Fox shows, call (213) 856-1520.

Mel Blanc's grave is one of the many attractions at Hollywood Memorial Park Cemetery.

43. HOLLYWOOD MEMORIAL PARK CEME-TERY, 6000 Santa Monica Boulevard (between Bronson and Van Ness Avenues)

Many of Hollywood's early greats (Rudolph Valentino, Mary Pickford, Cecil B. DeMille, Harry Cohn, Tyrone Power, and Douglas Fairbanks, Sr.) are buried here. So are Jayne Mansfield, Peter Finch, Peter Lorre, Carl "Alfalfa" Switzer, and John Huston. For years a mysterious veiled "Lady in Black" brought flowers to Rudolph Valentino's tomb on the anniversary of Valentino's death. The Jewish section of the cemetery features the graves of mobster Bugsy Siegel, as well as Mel Blanc, the voice of Bugs Bunny and Porky Pig, whose epitaph reads: "That's all folks." Visiting hours are 8:00 A.M. to 5:00 P.M. throughout the grounds. Maps of the stars' graves are available at the main entrance for those wishing to tour the site.

44. RALEIGH STUDIOS, 650 N. Bronson Avenue (on both the southeast and southwest corners of Melrose)

Raleigh may or may not be the oldest continually operating studio in Hollywood (KCET makes the same claim, and the dispute is probably over the word "continually"). In any event, it is a rental studio used primarily for television production, although commercials, feature films, and music videos are also filmed here. When the studio was called the Producers' Studio in the 1960s, Ronald Reagan hosted "Death Valley Days" here. Episodes from "The Life of Riley," "Superman," "Gunsmoke," "Perry Mason," and "Have Gun, Will Travel" were also filmed on the Raleigh lot. More recently it has been used for filming shows like "Roc," "Baby Talk" and "Amen." Not open to the public.

45. PARAMOUNT STUDIOS, 5555 Melrose Avenue

Paramount is the only major studio that has not fled Hollywood for the suburbs. One of its main attractions is its famous wrought-iron side gate, at the corner of Bronson Avenue and Marathon Street—which is not to be confused with the main gate on Melrose. The side gate was immortalized in *Sunset Boulevard* and has appeared in countless other movies.

The Paramount Studios gate.

Although the studio does not publicize their tour ("we do not want it to get too large or too disruptive; we do it more as a public service," says a studio spokesman), the studio does offer a two-hour walking tour of its lot. The tour, which starts at the side entrance of the studio at 860 N. Gower Street, is conducted three times daily, Monday through Friday, at 8:30 A.M., 11:00 A.M. and 2:00 P.M., and costs a reasonable $10. Visitors are walked through the back lot, shown how various studio depatments operate, and sometimes given the opportunity to watch rehearsals. The rehearsal-watching is not guaranteed. The chances of seeing a show being rehearsed are much greater in the late spring or summer, when shows are in production, and not possible at all when the shows are on hiatus, usually during the Christmas holiday and late spring. It is also possible to get tickets to see shows produced by Paramount by calling (213) 956-5575.

(Note: After driving past Paramount you have a number of options for additional touring. You can make a left turn onto Rossmore Avenue and do the Hancock Park/Wilshire District tour—or you can continue west on Melrose for about a mile and a half until you reach La Brea. Between La Brea and Fairfax is the world-famous Melrose Avenue shopping district, which is the only place in the world where you will find stores with names like Wacko, Condomania, Street Legal, and Retail Slut. Melrose is a popular hangout among yuppies and punk rockers. The television show "Melrose Place" sometimes films on Melrose Avenue; but do not go looking for the apartment building. It exists only on a studio backlot in the city of Santa Clarita, some thirty miles north of Los Angeles.

Also not on the map—and a few blocks out of the way—is another rental studio, Hollywood Center Studios, 1040 N. Las Palmas Avenue, located two blocks east of Highland Avenue and north of Melrose— before the Melrose shopping district. There is not much to see from the outside, but just about everything has filmed on the lot: features [*The Addams Family, Misery,* and *When Harry Met Sally*], games shows ["Jeopardy"], weekly television series ["I Love Lucy," "The Ozzie and Harriet Show," "The Burns and Allen Show," "Mr. Ed," and "The Beverly Hillbillies"], commercials, and music videos, including some by Michael Jackson. The studio does not offer a tour of its facilities.)

Yes, this is a restaurant: The Burger That Ate LA, located at 7624 Melrose Avenue.

CELEBRITIES WHO OWN HOMES IN HOLLYWOOD: No celebrities live in the Hollywood "flats", but a number live in the fashionable hills above Hollywood Boulevard. Penny Marshall, Beverly D'Angelo, Ken Kercheval, Bob Barker, Lou Diamond Phillips, Ruth Buzzi, Alyce Beasley, Rebecca De Mornay, Ken Berry and Howard Hesseman live in the prestigious Outpost Estates, by Outpost Drive. Kathleen Beller, Thomas Dolby, and Michelle Green live in Whitley Heights, a community north of Highland and east of Franklin Avenue (behind the Hollywood Studio Museum) where many of the stars of the silent era once lived. Marina Sirtis, Gates McFadden, Ned Beatty, Ione Skye, Pee-Wee Herman, Jason Priestly, Diane Keaton, Paul Winfield, Terrence Knox, Jim J Bullock, Peter Bonerz, Jodi Watley, and Neil Young have homes in "Hollywoodland"—the Hollywood Hills east of Highland Avenue. Lily Tomlin, Elvira, and Stevie Wonder live in Los Feliz, an exclusive neighborhood of grand older houses south of Griffith Park.

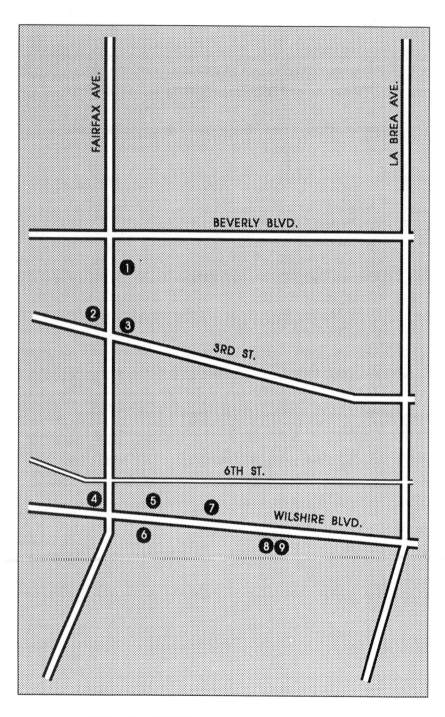

MAP 22   FAIRFAX AND THE MIRACLE MILE

☆ FAIRFAX AND
THE MIRACLE MILE

1. CBS TELEVISION CITY, 7800 Beverly Boulevard (at Fairfax Avenue)

CBS does not offer a tour of its facility, but tickets for "Family Feud," "Wheel of Fortune," "The Price is Right," and other programs airing on the network are available by calling (213) 852-2458. CBS also has a walk-up ticket booth open 9:00 A.M. to 5:00 P.M., where you can pick up tickets for shows filming that evening.

2. OLIVE, 119 S. Fairfax Avenue (across from Farmer's Market), (213) 939-2001

The restaurant, which is a major music industry hangout, is so trendy that it does not publish its phone number or have a sign advertising it. Not for those looking for a smoke-free atmosphere.

3. FARMER'S MARKET, 3rd Street and Fairfax Avenue, (213) 933-9211

Surprisingly, the *Los Angeles Times* placed Farmer's Market at the top of its list of the ten best places to spot celebrities in L.A. The *Times* claims that: "A wide spectrum of celebs is known to meander through the stalls, from John Malkovich and Michelle Pfeiffer to Mickey Rooney and Doris Day. The young crowd eats at Kokomos, the older ones are there to shop. The soap opera stars from CBS are there to grab lunch."

4. JOHNIE'S RESTAURANT, 6101 Wilshire Boulevard (at Fairfax Avenue), (213) 938-3521

The 1989 thriller *Miracle Mile* told the story of a musician and his girlfriend who learned of an impending nuclear strike and tried to escape Hollywood before the missiles hit. The musician in the movie, Anthony Edwards, learned of the attack at a phone booth outside this restaurant. (The booth was a prop added for the movie.)

5. LOS ANGELES COUNTY MUSEUM OF ART, 5905 Wilshire Boulevard, (213) 857-6000

The museum has appeared in several movies, including *L.A. Story,* in which Steve Martin, a real-life avid art collector, was the only one in a foursome to see a naked woman in a work of abstract art. In *The Player,* Cher and dozens of other celebrities, playing themselves, attended a gala studio event. Featuring some of the country's best art, the museum is worth a visit. The museum is closed on Mondays but is open Tuesdays through Thursdays from 10:00 A.M. to 5:00 P.M., Fridays from 10:00 A.M. to 9:00 P.M., and Saturdays and Sundays from 11:00 A.M. to 6:00 P.M.

6. MUTUAL BENEFIT LIFE BUILDING, 5900 Wilshire Boulevard

This 31-story building is the site from which Anthony Edwards desperately tried to arrange a helicopter get-away in *Miracle Mile.* The helicopter eventually landed on the roof of the building, and Edwards and Mare Winningham got as far as the La Brea Tar Pits across the street.

168

7. LA BREA TAR PITS AND THE GEORGE C. PAGE MUSEUM OF LA BREA DISCOVERIES, 5801 Wilshire Boulevard, (213) 857-6301

The Pits are pools of asphaltum and crude oil that have trapped more than 200 varieties of birds, mammals, plants, reptiles and insects, some dating back to prehistoric times.

8. WILSHIRE COURTYARD, 5750 and 5750 Wilshire Boulevard

Twin office buildings which house (in addition to banks and attorneys' offices) Mark Goodson Productions, Aaron Spelling Productions, DePasse Entertainment, and *Us* magazine.

9. HEADQUARTERS OF E! ENTERTAINMENT TELEVISION, 5670 Wilshire Boulevard

This is the corporate headquarters and production studios of the cable network, which presents news and features about the entertainment world and its major celebrities. The channel is available in 20 million American homes.

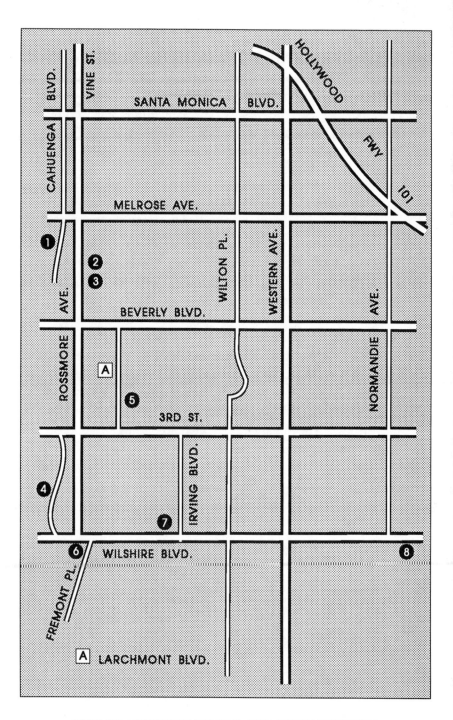

MAP 23 HANCOCK PARK & WILSHIRE DISTRICT

☆ HANCOCK PARK AND THE WILSHIRE DISTRICT

1. "HAPPY DAYS" HOME, 565 N. Cahuenga Avenue (south of Melrose Avenue)

Served as the Cunningham home in the long-running hit TV series "Happy Days."

2. FORMER HOME OF MAE WEST, 570 N. Rossmore Avenue

For 48 years (from 1932 until her death in 1980), Mae West lived in the penthouse of the Ravenswood Apartments.

3. EL ROYALE APARTMENTS, 450 N. Rossmore Avenue (at Rosewood Avenue)

For years a story circulated that John F. Kennedy stayed here during the 1960 Democratic National Convention in Los Angeles, even though his official campaign headquarters was at the Biltmore Hotel in downtown L.A. Sandra Griffin, the El Royale's property manager, checked into the stories, and reported that JFK did not stay at the El Royale, but stayed in room 301 at an apartment building (formerly a hotel, the Rossmore House) two doors down the street—at 522 N. Rossmore Avenue. The book *Johnny, We Hardly Knew Ye* by former JFK aides Kenneth P. O'Donnell and David F. Powers with Joe McCarthy, confirms this, stating that Powers found the hideaway apartment so JFK could "sleep and eat a quiet breakfast, away from the turmoil at the Biltmore."

Tour buses which drive past the El Royale can continue to note it as a point of interest, though. Several celebrities have lived there at one time or another, including former Columbia Pictures president Harry Cohn; William Frawley, who played Fred on "I Love Lucy;" George Raft; Loretta Young; and most recently, before buying a castle in Hollywood, actor Nicolas Cage. The lobby of the building was seen in *Switch* starring Ellen Barkin and in *Other People's Money*, where it served as Penelope Anne Miller's apartment.

4. FORMER NAT KING COLE HOME, 401 Muirfield Road

Cole bought this English Tudor mansion in 1948 as a wedding present for his bride, Maria, shocking and angering his WASPy neighbors, who were not used to having blacks around. According to *Lamparski's Hidden Hollywood*, by Richard Lamparski: "Larchmont residents called a property owners' meeting shortly after the Coles moved in. An attorney for the group summed up its feelings when he said that many of those present were born and raised in Larchmont: 'We are greatly disturbed at the prospect of having undesirables living here.' Cole responded: 'I'm relieved to hear how concerned you all are about your neighborhood. I feel exactly the same way. I'd like you all to know that if my wife or I see anyone undesirable in Larchmont we'll be the first to object. Thank you'" (Other notables who lived on Muirfield include Howard Hughes, whose first Los Angeles home was at 211; Buster Keaton, who owned a home at 543; and Dan Blocker who lived at 555 Muirfield Road.)

5. MRX PHARMACY, 150 N. Larchmont Boulevard

During the first two seasons of "MacGyver"—when the show was filmed in Los Angeles in 1985 and 1986—Richard Dean Anderson (MacGyver) lived in the loft above the pharmacy. Many of chase scenes from the Keystone Cop comedies were also filmed on Larchmont.

6. 119 FREMONT PLACE, between 4400 and 4500 Wilshire Boulevard

This was Michael Douglas and Kathleen Turner's home in *War of the Roses.* The house is in a gated community and is not visible from the street. (Fremont Place has always attracted celebrities. Muhammed Ali lived for years at 55 Fremont Place; Mary Pickford and her mother lived across the street at 56; and Cliff Robertson lived at 97 Fremont Place when the David Begelman scandal broke. Mick Jagger also lived on Fremont Place in the mid-1980s. Sylvester Stallone's house in *Rocky,* according to location manager Mike Alvarado, was also on this street.)

7. SITE OF THE "SUNSET BOULEVARD" MANSION (northwest corner of Wilshire and Irving Boulevards)

An office building with the address 4155 Wilshire Boulevard is now at this site, but in 1950 the mansion in which Gloria Swanson lived in the classic *Sunset Boulevard,* stood here. The mansion once belonged to billionaire J. Paul Getty and was also featured in *Rebel Without a Cause.*

8. AMBASSADOR HOTEL, 3400 Wilshire Boulevard

The Ambassador was once a Hollywood hot spot and is perhaps best known as the site where Robert F. Kennedy was assassinated while running for the presidency in 1968. The hotel closed in 1990 and is today used exclusively for location filming. American Film Location Company, which leases the Ambassador to filmmakers, would not provide any information about what has filmed there, but public records indicate that the Ambassador was L'Idiot Restaurant in *L.A. Story* (where maître d' Patrick Stewart cross-examined Steve Martin); Wrigley Field in *Opportunity Knocks* (Dana Carvey's bathroom scene); the setting for the downtown meeting between Robert DeNiro, playing a blacklisted writer, and his attorney Sam Wanamaker in *Guilty by Suspicion;* the hotel Meryl Streep stayed at in *Defending Your Life;* and both a Catskill resort and a glitzy Las Vegas showroom in Billy Crystal's *Mr. Saturday Night.* The Academy Awards were presented in the hotel's famous Cocoanut Grove six times between 1930 and 1943. In 1947 Marilyn Monroe started as a model at the Emmaline Snively's Blue Book Modeling Agency, located at the hotel.

JUST OFF THE MAP are a few sites which certainly are not must-sees for tourists who are in Los Angeles for just a short time, but which are worth pointing out if you happen to be driving east on Wilshire Boulevard on your way toward downtown. The first is the Bryson Apartment Hotel, located at 2701 Wilshire Boulevard, at the corner of Lafayette Park Place. The apartment was featured in Raymond Chandler's novel *The Lady of the Lake* and was where John Cusack lived in *The Grifters.* Just east of that is MacArthur Park,

174

which borders 6th and 7th Streets on the north, and Park View on the east and Alvarado Street on the west. Richard Harris immortalized the park in his hit song "MacArthur Park." The area is not one a tourist would go to; it is one of the more dangerous areas in town. Overlooking MacArthur Park, at 607 S. Park View Street (at the corner of Sixth Street), is the Park Plaza Hotel, which is constantly used as a film location. The hotel served as the setting for Ricardo Montalban's office in *The Naked Gun,* the party scene in *Less Than Zero,* Donald Sutherland's home in *Buffy and the Vampire Slayer,* and has also been used for the filming of *Bugsy, Newsies,* and *The Bodyguard.*

CELEBRITIES WHO LIVE IN HANCOCK PARK OR NEARBY: Dixie Carter and Hal Holbrook, Elizabeth Perkins, James Ingram, Richard Mulligan, Lou Rawls, George Takei, John Malkovich, Mayor Tom Bradley, and Mr. Blackwell.

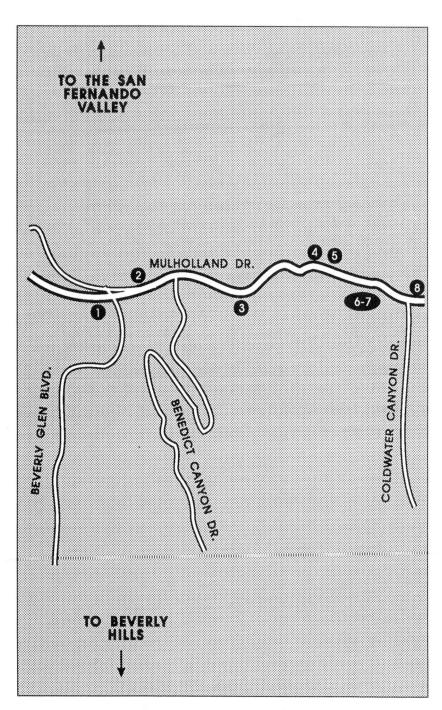

TO THE SAN
FERNANDO
VALLEY

MULHOLLAND DR.

BEVERLY GLEN BLVD.

BENEDICT CANYON DR.

COLDWATER CANYON DR.

TO BEVERLY
HILLS

MAP 24   HOLLYWOOD HILLS

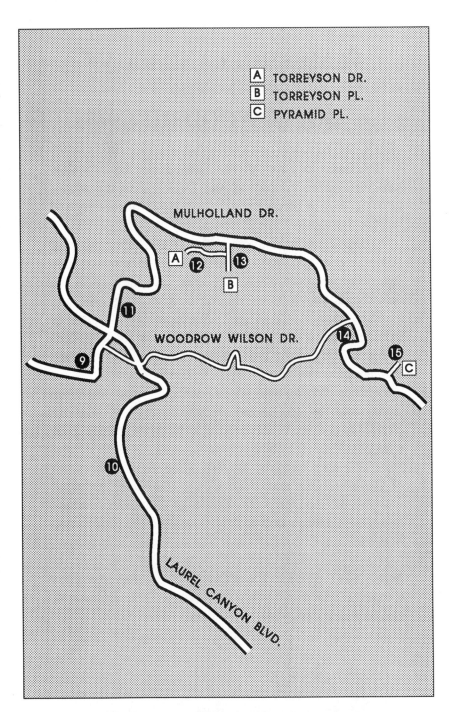

A TORREYSON DR.
B TORREYSON PL.
C PYRAMID PL.

MULHOLLAND DR.

A ⑫ B ⑬

⑪

WOODROW WILSON DR.

⑭

⑮ C

⑨

⑩

LAUREL CANYON BLVD.

MAP 25   HOLLYWOOD HILLS

☆ MULHOLLAND DRIVE AND THE HOLLYWOOD HILLS

A visit to Los Angeles would not be complete without a drive on Mulholland Drive—a windy mountain road which offers breathtaking views of the city and the San Fernando Valley, particularly at night.

Because it is so curvy, Mulholland demands your constant attention. If you make one little mistake, you can drive your car off a cliff—just like they do in the movies (although most of the cliff crash scenes are actually done in the Angeles National Forest north of Los Angeles. Mulholland is more famous for its scenes of lovemaking at the turn-off points which offer the best vantage points of the Valley.)

Since Mulholland does demand your attention, sightseeing by car is not recommended—if you are alone. Of course, if someone else is driving, keep your eyes posted for the following landmarks.

This tour starts by Beverly Glen Boulevard (north of Beverly Hills and Bel-Air) and continues eastward until Mulholland ends by Cahuenga Boulevard—which is north of Hollywood and just west of the Hollywood Freeway.

1. SANTO PIETRO'S PIZZA, 2954 Beverly Glen Centre, (310) 474-4349 (off Beverly Glen Boulevard, one-half block south of Mulholland)

Vanna White's husband, George Santo Pietro, owns this restaurant, which is often frequented by many of the celebrities who live on Mulholland. Warren Beatty met Annette Bening here.

2. MULHOLLAND ESTATES, 14111 Mulholland Drive (north side of street, between Beverly Glen Boulevard and Benedict Canyon Drive)

Exclusive gated community where Fred Dryer, Paula Abdul, Vanna White, and Wayne Gretzky are building homes. (Eagles star Don Henley lives in a house across the street. His home is not, however, visible from the street.)

3. BEVERLY PARK (north entrance by 13100 Mulholland Drive)

The most exclusive of the private communities in Los Angeles; it is where Magic Johnson, Sasha Stallone, Pia Zadora, Rod Stewart, Richard and Lili Zanuck, Alan Thicke, drummer Alex Van Halen, and Jon Peters have (or are building) homes.

4. HOME OF WARREN BEATTY, 13671 Mulholland Drive

This is not visible from the street.

5. FORMER HOME OF BRUCE WILLIS AND DEMI MOORE, 13511 Mulholland Drive

This is also not visible from the street.

6. JACK NICHOLSON'S HOME, 12850 Mulholland Drive

This is where, in Nicholson's absence, Roman Polanski seduced a 13-year-old model, leading to a 1977

Jack Nicholson's home on Mulholland Drive.

charge of unlawful sexual intercourse to which Polanski pleaded guilty. Polanski spent 42 days undergoing psychiatric observation at Chino State Prison; and then, to avoid further jail time, fled to Europe. He now lives in permanent exile in Paris, where he continues to make films.

7. MARLON BRANDO COMPOUND, 12900 Mulholland Drive

Brando had even worse trouble in this $4 million compound, which is located behind the same security gate as Nicholson's. On May 16, 1990, Brando's son Christian shot and killed Brando's daughter's lover, Dag Drollet. Christian later pleaded guilty to a charge of voluntary manslaughter and received a 10-year prison sentence. (Neither Nicholson's nor Brando's homes are visible from the street.)

8. THE SUMMIT, 12000 Mulholland Drive

Another gated community, although not as posh as Beverly Park. Fred Roggin, Ed McMahon, Anita Pointer, and Eddie van Halen and Valerie Bertenelli have homes here.

9. FORMER HOME OF RICK JAMES, 8115 Mulholland Terrace (just west of Laurel Canyon and north of Mulholland Drive)

In 1991 Grammy Award-winning singer Rick James, best known for his song "Super Freak," and his girlfriend, Tanya Anne Hijazi, were charged with imprisoning and torturing a 24-year-old woman at this house. Police charged that James met the woman at a party, offered to put her up at his house, and then threatened to kill her if she left. James allegedly tied her up, forced the victim to orally copulate Hijazi, and burned her with a crack cocaine pipe. James and his girlfriend were arrested by police in August 1991, and await trial as we go to press. (The late Ralph Bellamy lived down the street at 8173 Mulholland Terrace.)

10. SO-CALLED "HOUDINI ESTATE," 2398 Laurel Canyon Boulevard

Just off the map, about 7/10 of a mile south of Mulholland Drive are the ruins of an estate that several books on Hollywood identify as once belonging to Harry Houdini. About all that is left of the estate are servants' quarters, steps which led to an Italian villa once standing on the site, and a bridge that seemed to once connect the villa with the houses located across the street on Laurel Canyon Boulevard.

Since Houdini once vowed to return from the dead, psychics still hold seances on the property, and legends persist that two ghosts—Houdini's plus the ghost of a mysterious woman dressed in green lingerie—haunt the estate. Houdini worked on several silent films in Hollywood in 1919, but a leading Houdini expert, Manny Weltman, insists that Houdini never leased or owned the property, and that during his Hollywood stay he either stayed at a fellow magician's home or in a studio bungalow. Unfortunately, title searches of the property do not reveal who owned the estate before 1922. To protect itself against charges of false advertising, a real estate company that tried to sell the property recently advertised it as the "estate known as Harry Houdini's."

11. HOME OF "JEOPARDY!" HOST ALEX TREBEK, 7966 Mulholland Drive

Trebek, who turned 52 in 1992, lives here with his lovely wife Jean, who is 24 years his junior.

12. THE CHEMOSPHERE, 7776 Torreyson Drive (one block north of Mulholland Drive)

This is one of the most extraordinary houses in Southern California—if not the world. Shaped like an eight-sided flying saucer (and sometimes mistaken for one, particularly at night), the Chemosphere sits atop a single concrete post several hundred feet above Torreyson Drive. Brian DePalma used it in his 1984 film *Body Double* as the house where down-on-his-luck actor Craig Wasson (playing Jack Scully) becomes a pawn in a bizarre murder. To get to the house, the occupants have to either climb more than 100 steps or take a cable car from the garage, which is on street level, to the house's front door. The house was designed by the famed architect John Lautner, who also designed Bambi and Thumper's house in the James Bond film *Diamonds Are Forever*, as well as a house down the street at 7436 Mulholland that Mel Gibson brought down from its pedestal in *Lethal Weapon 2* (description follows). The best views of the Chemosphere are from the corner of Torreyson Drive and Flynn Ranch Road or from across the street at 7777 Torreyson Drive.

13. ERROL FLYNN'S "MULHOLLAND HOUSE," 3100 Torreyson Place

Flynn threw wild parties here and installed one-way mirrors so he and his friends could watch his houseguests making love. The house was later owned by Richard Dreyfuss, as well as Rick Nelson, who was the last person to live in the house before it was torn down. Recently the property—sans house—was sold to the president of New York Seltzer for $4 million.

14. "LETHAL WEAPON 2" FILMING SITE, 7436 Mulholland Drive

In the movie *Lethal Weapon 2*, Mel Gibson tied the pedestal of this house, designed by John Lautner, to a pickup truck, and brought the house down by driving away. Of course, the house was not really destroyed. The producers built two exact duplicates of the house—one on Stage 1 at Burbank Studios; the other in Newhall, 20 miles north of Los Angeles, and destroyed those instead. It was the house in Newhall which plummeted to the bottom of the hill. In the movie the house was the residence of the evil ambassador of South Africa. In real life it is owned by Los Angeles attorney David Grey.

15. HOUSE REPORTED TO BE ARSENIO HALL'S, 7430 Pyramid Place

Arsenio has denied published reports that he bought this historic estate, once owned by Rudy Vallee, even though the title is in the name of his management company and the *Los Angeles Times* has identified him as being the owner. He has also denied knowledge of construction of a monstrous tennis court on the grounds, even after more than 100 of his neighbors, including actors Martin Landau and Robert Carradine, successfully petitioned the City Board of Zoning Appeals to stop the construction. The house, north of Mulholland, is not visible from the street.

John Lautner's "Flying Saucer" in the Hollywood Hills.

185

OTHER CELEBRITIES WHO LIVE ON MUL-
HOLLAND DRIVE: Julian Lennon, Rennie Har-
lin, Shaun Cassidy, Richard Grieco, Burt
Reynolds, Rob Lowe, Robin Leach, and Maryam
D'Abo. Farrah Fawcett and Ryan O'Neal, Wilt
Chamberlain, Ed McMahon, Ernest Borgnine,
Anthony Gear, Sharon Stone, Anthony Perkins,
and Michael Dorn own homes just off Mulholland.
A number of celebrities also live in the Hollywood
Hills nearby: Dan Aykroyd, Brian Robbins and
Holly Robinson, Frank Zappa, Gena Rowlands,
Sally Kellerman, Lea Thompson, Justine Bateman,
Valeria Golino, Melanie Mayron, Cathy Guise-
wite, Morgan Fairchild, and Katey Sagal. Alan
Funt, Robert Hays, Richard Dreyfuss, Michael
Nader, Stevie Wonder, Gordon Thomson, Julia
Roberts, Paul Rieser, Burt Lancaster, and Susan
Ruttan own property on or just off Nichols
Canyon.

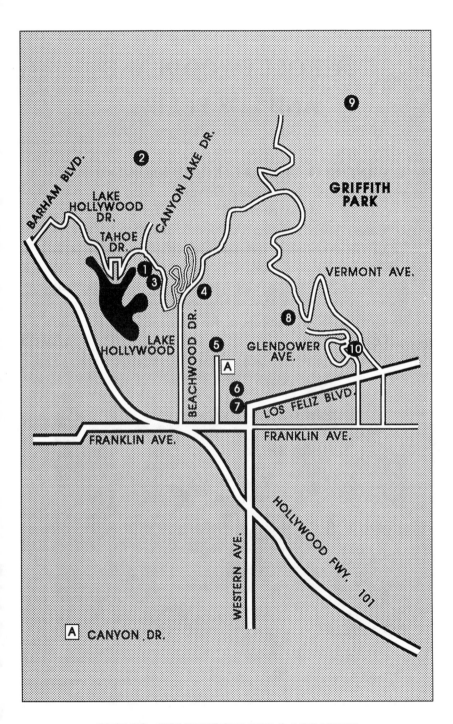

MAP 26   HOLLYWOODLAND & LOS FELIZ

☆ HOLLYWOODLAND AND LOS FELIZ

1. CASTILLO DEL LAGO, 6342 Mulholland Highway (corner of Canyon Lake Drive)

In 1993 Madonna paid $5 million for this 32-room, nine-story tall, Spanish-style colonial mansion. She also horrified neighbors by painting it deep red with alternating red and yellow horizontal stripes over the compound's retaining wall and bell tower. The odd color scheme only added to the home's colorful history. In past years it had reportedly been used as a bordello and gambling den.

This castle was Bugsy Siegel's gambling den in the 1930s.

188

According to Charles Lockwood's *The Guide to Hollywood and Beverly Hills*, the castle was used by mobster Bugsy Seigel in the 1930's and "fit Bugsy's security needs perfectly—or so he thought. The only entrance was through a courtyard near the bottom of the house at the end of a long, narrow, winding driveway. The police would never attack the house from this approach. Because of the house's unobstructed views, Bugsy's strong-armed men thought that they could see the police coming from all other directions. But they were wrong. One night the police stormed Castillo del Lago from a neighboring house, and Bugsy's gambling-den days were over, at least for a while." The best place to view the castle is from the hiking trail which runs along its side. (Incidentally, it is possible to hike from this castle to Wolf's Lair, described on the following page. The trail, which is about half a mile long, provides the best views of Lake Hollywood, which was featured in both *Chinatown* and *Earthquake*. In *Earthquake,* the reservoir's dam collapsed, and the ensuing flood swept away all the people and buildings in its path.)

2. HOLLYWOOD SIGN, atop Mt. Lee
The Hollywood Sign, which is probably more recognizable worldwide than the Statue of Liberty or the White House, is actually a giant billboard with letters over fifty feet high and thirty feet wide. It was originally constructed in 1923 as "Hollywoodland" to advertise homes sold by the Hollywoodland Realty Company (still in existence in Beachwood Canyon), and when the last four letters of "Hollywoodland" fell off, the sign became a symbol of the entertainment industry itself. Until recently, it was possible to hike to the sign from Mulholland Highway, which provides close-up views.

However, a gate has since been erected to discourage vandals and jumps by the potentially suicidal.

3. WOLF'S LAIR, 2869 Durand Drive

Efrem Zimbalist, Jr., and Doris Day are former tenants of this intriguing chateau, situated at the end of the hiking trail alongside Bugsy Siegel's gambling castle. The house was featured in the 1978 film *Return from Witch Mountain,* starring Bette Davis. Its original owner, Milton Wolf, died at the dining room table, leading to tales that this is one of L.A.'s many haunted houses.

4. "INVASION OF THE BODY SNATCHERS" FILMING SITE, corner Belden and Beachwood Drives

While some of the most memorable scenes in the original *Invasion of the Body Snatchers* were filmed in the town square of Sierra Madre, a small community just northeast of Pasadena (it was there that Kevin McCarthy and Dana Wynter hid from the pod people), the scenes of their escape were filmed at the corner of Beachwood and Belden Drives. The couple ran eastward up the hill on Belden Drive, and then up a flight of 148 steps actually located one block north of that intersection, at the corner of Beachwood and Woodshire Drives. The Beachwood Market, located at 2701 Belden Drive, decorates its walls with stills from the movie. The area is one of the most intriguing in Hollywood, and do not be surprised if you see famous faces in the Beachwood Market or the Village Coffee Shop.

5. BRONSON CAVES (at the end of Canyon Drive)

The Klingon prison camp in *Star Trek VI;* the Bat Cave in both the TV series "Batman" and the feature

190

film of the same name; the jungle island in the original *King Kong;* and numerous gunfights on "Gunsmoke," "Bonanza," and "Have Gun, Will Travel," were all filmed here. The caves are considered part of Griffith Park, but are not reachable through the park's main entrance. To see the caves, take Canyon Drive north until it ends, and hike a quarter of a mile up the trail to the right of the last parking lot.

What appears to be a castle at 2818 Hollyridge Drive (at the corner of Pelham) is actually a false front to a conventional hillside home. Down the street, though, at 3030 Hollyridge Drive, is a real castle that can be seen from the street.

6. NICOLAS CAGE'S CASTLE, 5647 Tryon Road

Cage paid $1.5 million in 1990 for this 5,367-square-foot castle which overlooks downtown L.A.

7. AMERICAN FILM INSTITUTE, 2021 N. Western Avenue (north of Franklin Avenue), (213) 856-7600

Established in 1967, the American Film Institute is a prestigious nonprofit national arts organization devoted to preserving film and encouraging new talent. Its Center for Advanced Film and Television Studies offers specialized postgraduate training in producing, directing, screenwriting, cinematography and production design. Seminars and workshops are led by some of the top figures in the entertainment industry.

8. GRIFFITH PARK OBSERVATORY, 2800 E. Observatory Road, (213) 664-1191

Griffith Park—which is the largest park in the United States—is sometimes referred to as an unofficial Hollywood back lot since so many productions are filmed there (over 1,000 in 1991). Says the park's film coordinator: "When companies need green space or a road that doesn't have buildings on it, they come here." Blast-off scenes in *The Rocketeer,* the final fight scenes in *Rebel Without a Cause,* and the opening scenes of *The Terminator* were filmed at the park observatory. A bust of James Dean stands on the planetarium's west front lawn.

The Griffith Park Observatory.

9. LOS ANGELES ZOO, 5333 Zoo Drive, (213) 666-4090

Seen in opening credits of the TV sitcom "Three's Company."

10. ENNIS-BROWN HOUSE, 2655 Glendower Avenue

In the 1991 feature *Grand Canyon,* Steve Martin, who played the obnoxious producer Davis, lived in this architecturally historic house, which was designed by Frank Lloyd Wright to resemble a Mayan temple. Martin's character was based on a real-life producer,

193

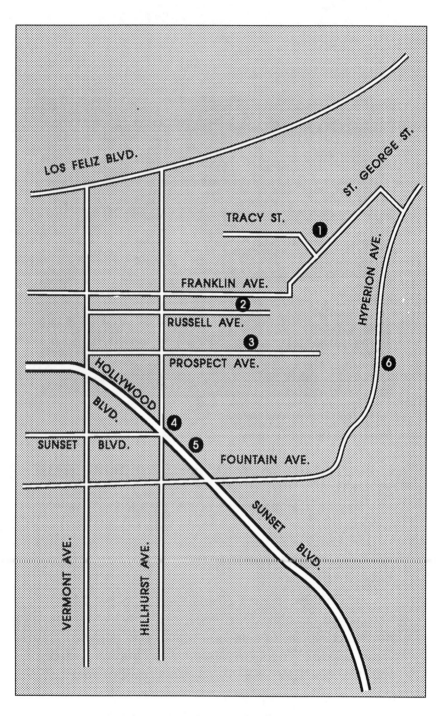

MAP 27 LOS FELIZ AND SILVER LAKE

Joel Silver, who, interestingly enough, happens to own two houses designed by Wright—one in South Carolina, the other a similarly-designed Mayan temple at 8161 Hollywood Boulevard, just north of the Sunset Strip. The Ennis-Brown House was also featured in *Blade Runner* (it served as Harrison Ford's home), *Karate Kid III* and *Black Rain*. Tours of the Ennis-Brown House are conducted on the second Saturdays of January, March, May, July, September and November. For tour information call (213) 660-0607.

---

1. JOHN MARSHALL HIGH SCHOOL, 3939 Tracy Street

This high school was Rydell High School in *Grease*, Dason High School in *Rebel Without a Cause*, and the schools used in the TV series "Mr. Novak" and the feature film *Buffy the Vampire Slayer*.

2. LYCÉE INTERNATIONAL DE LOS ANGELES, 4155 Russell Avenue

In *Jack the Bear*, starring Danny De Vito, the soccer field of this private school was transformed into a neighborhood in Oakland. Fox built twelve house facades, sidewalks and streets on this spot.

3. ABC TELEVISION CENTER, 4151 Prospect Avenue

The facility was originally built in 1915 by Vitagraph, one of the pioneer film companies, and was later bought by Warner Bros. in 1925. Warner turned the lot into a studio annex. In 1947 the facility was purchased by the just-created ABC Television Network.

Since then the broadcasting facility has been used to produce ABC network shows and is the home of KABC-TV (channel 7), the Los Angeles-owned and operated station of Capitol Cities/ABC Inc. The studio does not offer a public tour, but it is possible to see the taping of some ABC shows. For ticket information, call the ABC Show Ticket Hotline, (310) 520-1ABC, or write to ABC Guest Services, 4151 Prospect Avenue, Los Angeles, CA 90027.

4. SITE OF "BABYLON," 4500 Sunset Boulevard
Although long gone, the largest outdoors movie set ever built—the city of Babylon built for D. W. Griffith's 1916 silent film classic *Intolerance*—stood at this site for years.

5. KCET, 4401 Sunset Boulevard
One of the oldest continually used studios in Hollywood. Allied Artists, Monogram Pictures, and other long forgotten studios have made mostly "B" movies here ever since 1912. Since 1971 the site has been occupied by KCET, Southern Caliornia's public television station (channel 28). KCET doubled as KYOY in *L.A. Story* (Steve Martin played the daffy television weatherman here). Free one-hour tours are offered on Tuesdays and Thursdays.

6. SITE OF WALT DISNEY'S FIRST OFFICIAL STUDIO, 2701-39 Hyperion Avenue
The studio no longer exists (the Mayfair Food Market now occupies the land), but this is where *Snow White and the Seven Dwarfs* was produced as the first feature-length animated film. The site was declared a historic cultural monument by the city of Los Angeles in 1976.

☆ DOWNTOWN

1. DEPARTMENT OF WATER AND POWER, 111 N. Hope Street

The exterior was used as the 14th Precinct in "Cagney and Lacey," and the garage parking lot was used for shootout and chase scenes in *The Terminator*.

2. DOROTHY CHANDLER PAVILION, 135 N. Grand Avenue, (213) 972-7211

Home of the Los Angeles Philharmonic and the annual Academy Award presentations in most years since 1969. (Some of the recent awards—in 1988, 1989 and 1991—were held at the Shrine Auditorium in order to accommodate more members. The Shrine holds twice as many people, but is not as elegant as the marble and black-glass Pavilion. The Academy has decided in the future to rotate the Awards ceremony: three years at Dorothy Chandler, and the fourth at the Shrine.)

3. LOS ANGELES COUNTY COURTHOUSE, 111 N. Hill Street (extends from Grand to Hill)

Art Buchwald and producer Alain Bernheim successfully pursued a breach-of-contract suit against Paramount Pictures in this court when they were not compensated for their idea, which was appropriated for the Eddie Murphy film, *Coming to America*.

4. CRIMINAL COURTS BUILDING, 210 W. Temple Street (at Broadway)

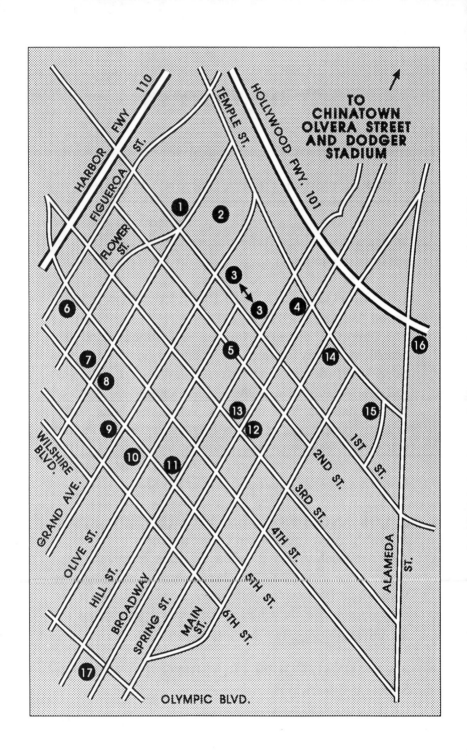

MAP 28 DOWNTOWN

5. SECOND STREET TUNNEL (between Hill and Figueroa Streets)

Used frequently in movie chase scenes—including *The Terminator*.

6. WESTIN BONAVENTURE, 404 S. Figueroa Street, (213) 624-1000

In the 1993 feature *In the Line of Fire*, Clint Eastwood played a Secret Service agent assigned to protect a president during a campaign stop here. The futuristic-looking hotel was also featured in the opening episode of "Moonlighting" and has appeared in *Blue Thunder, Ruthless People, Mr. Mom, Rainman, The Poseidon Adventure*, and *Lethal Weapon 2*. The Bona-Vista Lounge on the 35th floor is where the daffy waitresses in the sitcom "It's a Living" worked.

7. "LA LAW" BUILDING, 444 S. Flower Street

While this building is best known as the building seen in TV's "LA Law," its offices have also been used for *Baby Boom, Gotcha!* (where it served as CIA headquarters), and *Beverly Hills Cop II* (Gilbert Gottfried's scenes were filmed here).

8. FIRST INTERSTATE BANK BUILDING, 633 W. 5th Street

In *Life Stinks*, this was the office of Mel Brooks, who played Goddard Bolt, a developer who accepts a rival's challenge to try to survive for one month on Skid Row.

9. BILTMORE HOTEL, 506 S. Grand Street (at Fifth Street), (213) 624-1011; in California (800) 252-0175

Since it opened in 1923, the Biltmore has hosted kings, presidents, Hollywood celebrities and virtually every major league baseball team. In 1960 John F. Kennedy set up the official headquarters for the Democratic National Convention in suite 8315, and it was here that JFK and his brother Bobby decided on Lyndon Baines Johnson as JFK's running mate. A few years later, the Beatles, who had been mobbed by fans during their first U.S. tour, secretly helicoptered to the hotel's rooftop and hid at the Biltmore until moving to another location.

Over the last 20 years at least 300 feature films, television programs, and commercials have been filmed at the hotel. The Crystal Ballroom served as the setting for the bookie joint in *The Sting,* the fight arena in *Rocky III,* the prom scene in *Pretty in Pink* and the banquet scene in *Alien Nation,* the singing scenes in *The Fabulous Baker Boys,* and the slime scenes in *Ghostbusters. Vertigo* used the 11 flights of ornate, wrought-iron back stairs to create its dizzying scenes; and scenes from *Bugsy* were filmed at the Biltmore Health Club. The Biltmore was also the setting of eight early Academy Award ceremonies: in 1931, 1935 through 1939, and 1941 and 1942. Delta Burke and Gerald McRaney got married here in 1989.

10. REX IL RISTORANTE, 617 S. Olive Street, (213) 627-2300

In *Pretty Woman,* Julia Roberts accidentally flipped her escargot here. The eatery was also featured in *Bugsy* (where the restaurant was transformed into a New York clothing shop), *Memoirs of an Invisible Man* and *Final Analysis.*

11. TITLE GUARANTEE AND TRUST BUILDING, 411 W. 5th Street (at Hill Street, across from Pershing Square)

The exterior of this Art Deco building was the *Los Angeles Tribune* in the television show "Lou Grant." Today the Spanish-language *La Opinion* has offices there.

12. BRADBURY BUILDING, 304 S. Broadway (at 3rd Street)

This building was the site of Harrison Ford's home in *Blade Runner* and the setting of several television and movie private eye melodramas, including *Chinatown*. Sam Hall Kaplan, L.A.'s premier architectural critic, writes: "With its magical interior court bathed in light filtered through a glass roof and ornate ironwork and reflected off glazed yellow brick walls, the 1893 structure is one of the city's architectural treasures." (Note: In this part of town, bring plenty of quarters to fend off the panhandlers.)

13. MILLION DOLLAR THEATER, 307 S. Broadway

This architecturally intriguing movie palace was built by showman Sid Grauman in 1917, five years before he built the Egyptian Theater in Hollywood and ten years before he built the Chinese Theater.

14. CITY HALL, 200 N. Spring Street

"City Hall," writes *Los Angeles Times* researcher Cecilia Rasmussen, "has starred in more movies and television series than most Hollywood actors." Perhaps best known as the *Daily Planet* in the popular 1950s television series "Superman," City Hall, inside and out,

Los Angeles City Hall.

has been seen in *It Seems Like Old Times, 48 Hours, Another 48 Hours, Die Hard II, Dragnet,* and *Ricochet.* "Although it was destroyed by Martians in *War of the Worlds,*" Rasmussen notes, "it somehow survived to portray the U.S. Capitol in *The Jimmy Hoffa Story* and the Vatican in "The Thorn Birds" . . . You might have caught a glimpse of City Hall in the series 'Kojak,' 'Cagney and Lacey,' 'The Rockford Files,' 'Matlock,' 'Hill Street Blues,' 'LA Law,' 'Equal Justice,' 'The Trials of Rosie O'Neill,' and 'The Big One: The Great Los Angeles Earthquake.'"

15. PARKER CENTER, 150 N. Los Angeles Street
Headquarters for the Los Angeles Police Department. Seen in numerous television cop shows, most notably "Dragnet."

16. UNION STATION, 800 N. Alameda Street, (213) 683-6987
Union Station has been featured in *Grand Canyon, Blade Runner, Guilty by Suspicion, Bugsy, The Way We Were, Criss Cross*, several television series (including "Unsolved Mysteries," which often uses the station for Robert Stack's narratives), and of course, the 1950 movie *Union Station* starring William Holden. (Although there is a brief establishing shot of the station in *Silver Streak*, that movie was mostly filmed in Canada. The film required several stunts, and the station's management company does not grant filming permission to filmmakers who use on-site stunt work.)

17. HERALD EXAMINER BUILDING, 1111 S. Broadway
After the *Los Angeles Herald Examiner* went out of business in 1989, a location company, Hollywood Locations, moved in, and the building is now used exclusively as a location site for television shows and movies such as *V.I. Warshawski*. The exterior of the building was used as the police station in Clint Eastwood's *The Rookie*. The building itself is one of Los Angeles' most intriguing architectural landmarks. It was designed by Julia Morgan, the pioneering architect whose design so pleased William Randolph Hearst that he commissioned her to build his oceanside mansion in Santa Monica and his castle at San Simeon.

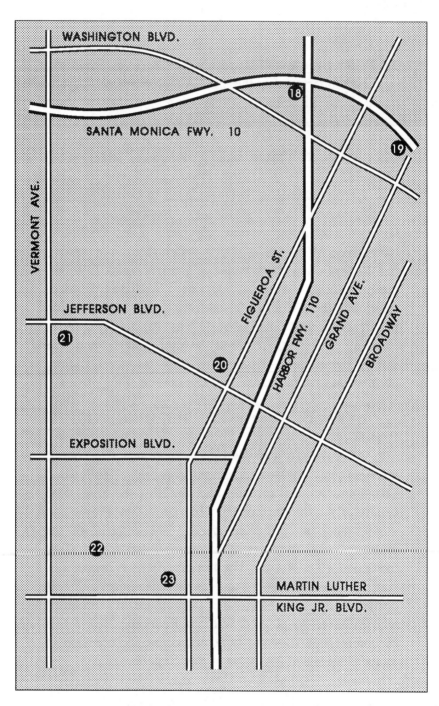

MAP 29 DOWNTOWN

18. C.H.I.P.S. HEADQUARTERS, 777 W. Washington Boulevard

The exterior of the Central Los Angeles office of the California Highway Patrol was used in the television show "C.H.I.P.S."

19. OLYMPIC AUDITORIUM, 1801 S. Grand Avenue (south of 10 and east of 110)

Many of Sylvester Stallone's boxing scenes in *Rocky* were filmed here.

The Shrine Auditorium.

20. SHRINE AUDITORIUM, 649 W. Jefferson Boulevard

The largest theater in the United States, the Shrine has been the site of the ceremonies for the Academy Awards, the Grammys, the American Music Awards, the MTV Awards and other shows. In the original *King Kong,* the gorilla was paraded in front of the auditorium and broke away from his chains. Goldie Hawn appeared from under a stage in *Foul Play,* and extras danced bear-chested for Oliver Stone during a concert filmed for his movie *The Doors.* The Shrine was also the site where Michael Jackson's hair caught on fire during the filming of a Pepsi commercial.

21. USC SCHOOL OF CINEMA AND TELE-VISION, 850 W. 34 Street (by Jefferson Boulevard and McClintock Avenue)

USC is widely considered to be one of the premier film schools in the country. Its film school is modeled after a Hollywood studio, and includes sound stages, screening rooms, classrooms and administrative offices. Alumni include "Star Wars" creator George Lucas; John Singleton, the Academy Award-nominated director and writer of *Boyz on the Hood;* Phillip Joanou, director of *Final Analysis;* Michael Lehmann, director of *Hudson Hawk, Heathers,* and *Meet the Applegates;* and Amanda Silver, screenwriter of *The Hand That Rocks the Cradle.* (USC's Rod Dedeaux baseball field doubled as the spring training diamond in *Mr. Baseball.* Other films shot on campus include *Cocoon,* which was filmed at the USC swimming pool; *The Graduate; Gross Anatomy; Wiseguys; The Hunchback of Notre Dame; House Party II;* and *Soul Man.)*

22. LOS ANGELES MEMORIAL COLISEUM, 3911 S. Figueroa Street

The Coliseum is the only arena that has hosted two Olympic games (1932 and 1984), two Super Bowls (1967 and 1972), a World Series (1959), and a Papal visit (Pope John Paul II in 1987). The opening and closing scenes of *The Last Boy Scout* were filmed here, as were the climactic scenes in *Black Sunday*. The Coliseum now offers group guided tours; call (213) 748-6136, extension 399, for information.

23. LOS ANGELES MEMORIAL SPORTS ARENA, 3939 S. Figueroa Street

Built in 1959, the Sports Arena hosts over 200 events each year, including the games of the NBA's Los Angeles Clippers and USC's men's and women's basketball teams. In 1960 John F. Kennedy was nominated for the presidency at the Democratic National Convention held here. Some of the fight scenes in *Rocky* were filmed at the Sports Arena.

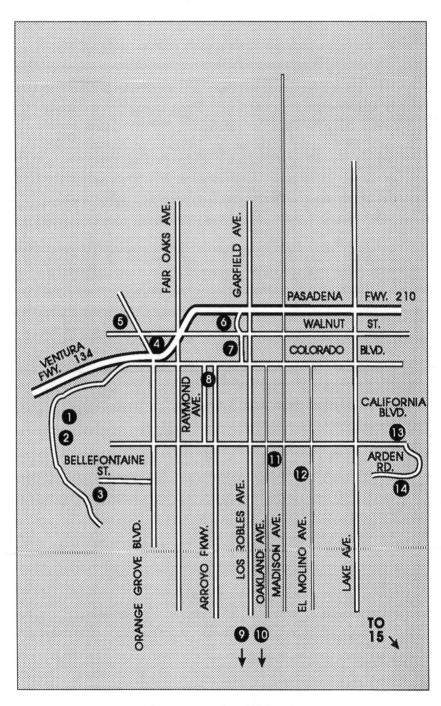

MAP 30 PASADENA

☆ PASADENA

1. THE INCORRECTLY IDENTIFIED "BATMAN MANSION," 160 S. San Rafael Avenue (south of Colorado Avenue)

This extraordinary three-story Tudor mansion has been cited in other tour books as the house used as the Wayne Manor in the 1960s television series, "Batman." However, Tonie Carnes, a researcher for the Pasadena Historical Society, discovered that the real Bat House was actually down the street a few blocks at 380 S. San Rafael Avenue. 160 S. San Rafael Avenue is not without its significance, though; it was used as a mansion in *Mobsters,* and as Sylvester Stallone's home in *Rocky V.*

2. THE REAL "BATMAN MANSION," 380 S. San Rafael Avenue

Unfortunately, the real Bat Mansion is not visible from the street. Neighbors say that the frequent filming at this mansion has sometimes created a carnival-like atmosphere on the street. The house, known to location scouts as Dr. Oh's (the doctor owns it), also served as Kenneth Branaugh's home in *Dead Again.*

3. MAYFIELD SENIOR SCHOOL, 500 Bellafontaine Street

One of Pasadena's most popular location sites (mostly for television series, movies of the week, soap operas and commercials), the private all-girls Catholic school was seen in the Disney musical *Newsies,* and in *Sneakers,* starring Robert Redford and Robert Duvall. (Behind the school, on Bellafontaine Terrace, is the house seen in the TV series "Valerie" starring Valerie Harper, in 1986. When Harper was replaced by Sandy Duncan the following year, the program became "Valerie's Family," and then "The Hogan Family," which aired on NBC, and then CBS, until 1990.)

4. FENYES MANSION, 470 W. Walnut Street (corner of Orange Grove), (818) 577-1660
Now the permanent home of the Pasadena Historical Society, this mansion was one of two mansions used in Hal Ashby's 1979 feature *Being There.* (The other was the Fenyes Mansion at 430 Madeline Avenue—now the home of the Red Cross.) In the movie, Peter Sellers played the caretaker whose ignorance was mistaken for profundity. Scenes from *Newsies* were also filmed there.

5. GAMBLE HOUSE, 4 Westmoreland Place (half a block north of the Fenyes Mansion, on a small, poorly marked side street just west of and reachable from Orange Grove)
In the *Back to the Future* movies, Christopher Lloyd ("Doc") lived in this house. It is an internationally recognized architectural landmark, a product of the turn-of-the-century Arts and Crafts movement. For tour hours, call (818) 793-3334.

6. PASADENA PUBLIC LIBRARY, 285 E. Walnut Street
The San Francico library in which Goldie Hawn worked in *Foul Play* was actually filmed here. Jeff Daniels did research here in *Arachnophobia.*

The Gamble House in Pasadena, where Christopher Lloyd lived in *Back to the Future*.

7. PASADENA CITY HALL, 100 N. Garfield Avenue

Used by the producers of the first two *Beverly Hills Cop* movies as exterior of Beverly Hills City Hall. (Filming permits cost less in Pasadena than in Beverly Hills.) The City Hall has also been used in television commercials as a stand-in for Buckingham Palace, and in the movie *Patton* as a French castle.

8. CASTLE GREEN APARTMENTS, 99 S. Raymond Avenue (corner of Green Street)

One of Pasadena's premier resort hotels before the turn of the century, the Castle Green is a popular location site because of its unusual Middle Eastern architecture. The outside of the building was used as the Hotel de Nacional in *Bugsy*, as a Russian consular office in San Francisco in *Sneakers,* and as a restaurant in *The*

Marrying Man. It was where "the sting" took place in *The Sting,* and was a location site in *Wild at Heart* and in *Sinatra.* Public tours are conducted twice a year—usually in April and in December—by Pasadena Heritage and the residents of the Castle Green. For further information call the Castle Green at (818) 793-0359.

9. "BENSON MANSION," 1365 S. Oakland Avenue

The exterior of this house was used as the Governor's mansion on the popular television series "Benson," which aired from 1979 to 1986.

10. "BEVERLY HILLBILLIES" MOVIE HOUSE, 1284 S. Oakland Avenue

Used for exterior shots of *The Beverly Hillbillies* movie. Interior scenes were filmed in four different mansions in Beverly Hills.

11. "DENNIS THE MENACE" HOUSE, 830 S. Madison Avenue

This is the house seen in Jay North's television series, which aired from 1959 to 1963.

12. "FATHER OF THE BRIDE" HOUSE, 843 S. El Molino Avenue

Although Steve Martin's narrative in the 1991 remake of *Father of the Bride* identified Steve Martin and Diane Keaton's residence as located in San Marino, the house was actually located in Pasadena, a few blocks north of San Marino (which discourages film-making by making their permits more expensive). The producers considered the house to be almost a character in the story. They looked for a house in an old-fashioned, idealized community—and considered this white clapboard residence perfect.

13. CALIFORNIA INSTITUTE OF TECHNOLOGY, 1201 E. California Boulevard (between Hill and Wilson Avenues)

Cal Tech would rather be known for its inventions (the seismograph and Richter scale); its scientific discoveries (its labs discovered anti-matter, quasars, quarks, the nature of the chemical bond, and the left brain-right brain hemispheres); its illustrious faculty and alumni (over 21 Nobel Laureates); and its consistent ranking as one of the top research universities in the world. Of course, since it is so close to Hollywood, Cal Tech occasionally shows up on the silver screen. The Athenaeum—a faculty dining club originally conceived as a meeting place for scholars — appeared in both *Beverly Hills Cop I* and *II*. In the first film it was the private club Eddie Murphy conned his way into, resulting in a fight in which Murphy threw Jonathan Banks across a buffet table. In *Beverly Hills Cop II*, the Athenaeum was used again as the site of the movie's villain-infested Beverly Hills Shooting Club. Cal Tech exteriors were viewed in *Real Genius, The War of the Roses, Funny About Love,* and *The Witches of Eastwick.*

14. "THE CARRINGTON MANSION," 1145 Arden Road

This is not the house seen in the opening credits of "Dynasty" (that one is located in the San Francisco suburb of Woodside). It is, however, the one that was used for the garden and pool shots (including Joan Collins' famous fights with Linda Evans) and for close-up outdoor scenes with the actors. The 20,000-

The oft-filmed Morton Mansion in Pasadena, seen in the popular
TV series "Dynasty."

214

square-foot mansion, Arden Villa, has been a frequent filming site, dating back to the 1933 Marx Brothers' classic *Duck Soup.* According to owner Charles Morton, who handles filming and corporate affair rentals, Arden Villa has appeared in at least 200 productions since 1980, including four television movies about the Kennedys, "Nixon's Last Days," several episodes of "Hart to Hart," "Flamingo Road," and Charles Bronson's *Death Wish.* The house also served as the Knight Rider Foundation in the TV show "Knight Riders."

15. THE HUNTINGTON LIBRARY, ART COLLECTIONS, AND BOTANICAL GARDENS, 1151 Oxford Road, San Marino, (818) 405-2141

This museum features 18th and 19th century British and French art, rare books and manuscripts, and 150 acres of botanical gardens. It was also the site of Robert and Anna's wedding in "General Hospital" and was seen in *Coming to America, MacArthur, War and Remembrance* and other features and television movies.

JUST OFF THE MAP, in South Pasadena, are a number of homes filmed in movies and television series. The Philadelphia house that Ken Olin and Patricia Wettig supposedly lived in on "Thirtysomething" was actually located at 1710 Bushnell Avenue in South Pasadena. Owner Donna Potts told a reporter that a location scout just came to the door one day before filming began and later offered a contract to the family. The house directly across the street—at 1711 Bushnell—was both the 1955 house where Lea Thompson and her family took in Michael J. Fox in *Back to the Future,* and Fox's home in *Teen Wolf.* In the *Back to*

215

the Future series, 1711 served as Crispin Glover's home, 1705 as Elisabeth Shue's, and 1809 as Thomas Wilson's. 1621 and 1615 Bushnell were both used as Bill Cosby's home in *Ghost Dad.* One block west, at 1632 Fletcher, is Patricia Wettig and Timothy Busfield's house in "Thirtysomething." Another block west of that is Milan Avenue, where Charles Grodin lived in *Beethoven* (at 1405). The house in "Family" is on the 600 block of Milan. In South Pasadena's historic business district is Carrow's Restaurant (815 S. Fremont Avenue), where Linda Hamilton, playing Sarah Connor, waitressed in *The Terminator.* Down the street, at 1518 Mission Street, is L. L. Balk Hardware—the hardware store where Fox worked at in *Teen Wolf.* Around the corner from L. L. Balk is the Rialto Theater, at 1023 S. Fair Oaks Avenue. It was at the Rialto that Tim Robbins, playing studio executive Griffin Mill in Robert Altman's 1992 feature *The Player,* met Vincent D'Onofrio, who played David Kahane, the writer whom Robbins thought was sending him threatening postcards. In the movie Robbins killed D'Onofrio behind the theater.

Also off the map—in the western section of Pasadena (just north of the Gamble House and south of the Rose Bowl) is Brookside Park, which was used extensively in "The Bionic Woman." In *High Anxiety,* one of the movies filmed at the park, there is a scene in which Mel Brooks paid homage to Hitchcock's movie *The Birds.* In the scene Brooks was drenched by bird droppings.

Between Pasadena and Glendale is the community of Eagle Rock, home of Occidental College. The college played California University in the TV series "Beverly Hills 90210."

216

CELEBRITIES WHO LIVE IN PASADENA: Barbara Babcock, Jessica Lange, Delta Burke and Gerald McRaney, Barbi Benton, and Orel Hershiser. Annie Potts lives in Glendale, another suburb of Los Angeles which is located between Pasadena and Burbank, and Kevin Costner lives in LaCanada-Flintridge, another suburb northeast of Glendale.

The Walsh family home in the popular television series "Beverly Hills 90210" is actually located at 1675 East Altadena Drive in Altadena, about four miles northeast of downtown Pasadena and a good forty minutes' drive from Beverly Hills.

The Queen Anne cottage seen in the television series "Fantasy Island" is located at the Los Angeles State and County Arboretum, at 301 N. Baldwin Avenue in Arcadia, no more than a ten-minute drive southeast of downtown Pasadena. The arboretum is a 127-acre botanical park which features exotic trees and shrubs arranged by their continent of origin. The opening sequence of "Fantasy Island" included stock footage of an airplane landing on the lake and Herve Villechaise's character, Tatoo, ringing the bell in the cottage tower, yelling "De plane, de plane." The producers actually only filmed a few episodes at the Arboretum, and then constructed a replica on the studio lot. The Arboretum has appeared in well over 200 television episodes and films, including eight Tarzan movies, *The African Queen, The Road to Singapore*, and other movies with jungle settings. For hours, call (213) 681-8411.

219

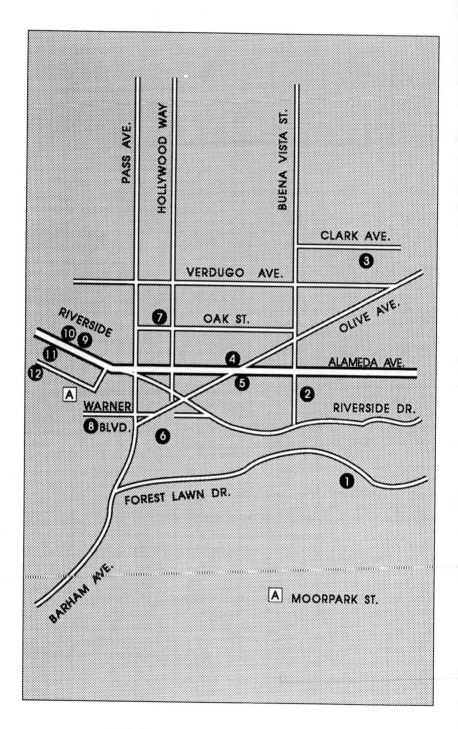

MAP 31   BURBANK AND TOLUCA LAKE

☆ BURBANK AND TOLUCA LAKE

1. FOREST LAWN MEMORIAL PARK HOLLY-WOOD HILLS, 6300 Forest Lawn Drive

This huge cemetery is the final resting place of Lucille Ball, Gene Roddenberry, Redd Foxx, Bette Davis, Andy Gibb, Jack Webb, Buster Keaton, Stan Laurel, Liberace, Ozzie Nelson, and Sammy Davis, Jr. Park maps are available at the front gates, but they do not show the locations of the stars' graves. A book published in 1989, *Permanent Californians: An Illustrated Guide to the Cemeteries of California* by Judi Culbertson and Tom Randall, does. That book also covers celebrity graves at Forest Lawn Glendale, 1712 S. Glendale Avenue, where many other luminaries are buried and where Ronald Reagan married Jane Wyman on January 27, 1940, at the Wee Kirk o' the Heather Church.

2. DISNEY STUDIOS, 500 S. Buena Vista Street

Since 1940, this has been the headquarters of Disney Studios, a company whose movies are loved by children—and whose allegedly tight-fisted business dealings are less loved by writers, producers and agents. In a recent *Vanity Fair* article, journalist Peter J. Boyer called Disney "a place so reviled that even its architecture inspires nasty rumors, such as the apocryphal story that architect Michael Graves arranged the drainage system in the Disney headquarters building in such a way that the huge sculpted Seven Dwarfs atop the edifice would seem to be peeing on Disney executives whenever it rained.'' Boyer also called Disney ''a place so tough in its dealings with the outside, so rigidly demanding of its own people, that it has earned an unlovely nickname that will be hard to erase. They call it Mouschwitz.'' Heading Mouschwitz (or Duckau's) movie division is Jeffrey Katzenberg, a negotiator so tough that actor Alec Baldwin once called him the eighth Dwarf: ''Greedy.''

The Disney administration building.

Of course, those who run Disney know that most people will not care how they treat the people who work with or for them, and will more likely associate Disney with its wonderful fairy tale movies such as *Snow White, Fantasia, The Little Mermaid,* and *Beauty and the Beast,* as well as its famous television shows: "Zorro," "Dragnet," and "The Wonderful World of Disney." The studio, apparently not wishing to compete with Disneyland, which is in Anaheim, more than thirty miles south of Burbank, does not offer a tour of its facilities.

3. BURROUGHS HIGH SCHOOL, 1920 Clark Avenue

One of the high schools used in filming the Emmy Award-winning "The Wonder Years." Ron Howard and Debbie Reynolds are Burroughs alumni.

4. DICK CLARK PRODUCTIONS, 3003 W. Olive Avenue

These are the offices of Clark's production company, which produces the American Music Awards, the Golden Globe Awards, the Academy of Country Music Awards, "New Year's Rockin' Eve," movies made for television and game shows. No tours. (Note: If you have ever wanted to take a side trip to beautiful downtown Burbank, just take Olive Avenue north. It is every bit as exciting as Johnny Carson says.)

5. NBC STUDIOS, 3000 W. Alameda Avenue

NBC is the only television network which offers a tour of its studios. It is also possible to see a taping of "The Tonight Show" and other shows filmed at the studio. The studio's ticket counter opens at 8:00 A.M. and distributes tickets for shows that tape for that

NBC Studios in Burbank.

evening. Ticket requests are also honored by mail if you write to the studio with the name of the show and enclose a self-addressed stamped envelope. NBC's ticket information number is (818) 840-3537.

6. WARNER BROS. STUDIOS, 4000 Warner Boulevard

Warner Bros., which has been headquarted here since 1929, offers a two-hour tour of its back lot and studio facilities. The tour, Warner spokespersons point

224

out, "is not a charade created for mass audiences" (an obvious jab at Universal Studios' tour), "but is, in fact, designed for small groups—no more than 12 persons—so that they may learn about the various components that go into the making of a film." On the day the author took the tour, he was treated to Marlee Matlin rehearsing scenes for the television show "Reasonable Doubts," an orchestra rehearsing a song for the 1992 Disney animated movie *Aladdin*, and a walk

An aerial view of Warner Bros.

through the prop department. Seeing a television show being filmed—or seeing scenes being rehearsed—is not guaranteed. The tour costs $25.00. No one under 10 is admitted. For tour information call (818) 954-1744.

7. WARNER BROS. RANCH FACILITIES, 3701 W. Oak Street

Behind the walls of this 40-acre back lot are sound stages and movie sets which include the facade of "The Partridge Family" house, Danny Glover's house in the *Lethal Weapon* series, Garp's house in *The World According to Garp,* and streets used in countless movies. The back lot is only sometimes shown during the Warner Bros. tour and is not otherwise open to the public.

8. "SCARECROW AND MRS. KING" HOUSE, 4247 Warner Boulevard

The exterior of this Cape Cod house was used as Kate Jackson and Beverly Garland's home in the television series "Scarecrow and Mrs. King."

9. PATY'S RESTAURANT, 10001 Riverside Drive, (818) 760-9164

A good spot to catch a glimpse of celebrities who work at nearby studios.

10. PORTRAIT OF A BOOKSTORE, 10061 Riverside Drive, (818) 769-3853

In the 1991 thriller *Ambition,* Lou Diamond Phillips played an aspiring writer who managed this bookstore and tried to manipulate a paroled convict into committing another crime so he could write a book about it. The store, which is Gore Vidal's favorite in Los

Angeles, does a brisk business with the nearby studios and has an impressive celebrity clientele. Delta Burke once spent $1,000 here on Christmas presents. The owners are producer Frank von Zerneck ("Gore Vidal's Billy the Kid" and "Portrait of a Centerfold") his wife, Julie, who was the original Heather on "General Hospital," and their children, Frank Jr. and Danielle, who are both actors.

11. RUBBER BOOTS, 10112 Riverside Drive, (818) 766-6666

Gift shop owned by Angela Cartwright, who played Angela on "Make Room for Daddy." Specializes in whimisical gifts, including candles, soaps, imported jewelry and toys.

12. HOME OF BOB HOPE, 10346 Moorpark Street

CELEBRITIES WHO LIVE IN TOLUCA LAKE: Jonathan Winters, Joanne Worley, Denzel Washington, Park Overall, Charles Haid, Henry Winkler, Markie Post, Andy Griffith, Alan Thicke, Garry Marshall, Rick Dees, and John Ratzenberger. Sandra Bernhard lives just outside the unofficial boundaries of Toluca Lake (which encompasses parts of North Hollywood and Burbank) in a surprisingly plain home in North Hollywood. Former residents of Toluca Lake include Bing Crosby, Al Jolson, Amelia Earhart, Moe Howard of "The Three Stooges," Frank Sinatra, William Holden, and W. C. Fields.

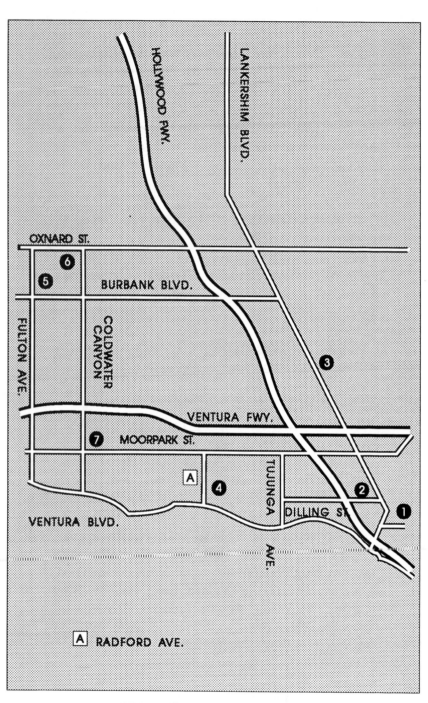

MAP 32 UNIVERSAL CITY, NORTH HOLLYWOOD, & STUDIO CITY

☆ UNIVERSAL CITY, NORTH HOLLYWOODAND STUDIO CITY

1. UNIVERSAL STUDIOS HOLLYWOOD, 100 Universal City Plaza, (818) 508-9600

As a tourist attraction, Universal Studios Hollywood

The *Psycho* House, seen on the Universal Studios Tour.

ranks second in Southern California only to Disneyland. In fact, it is so popular that the theme park actually makes more money every year for Universal than its movies. Universal offers stunt shows, technical attractions, and a tram tour through Universal's back lot (the largest in the world), where hundreds of movies and television programs have been filmed. The Bates Motel, seen in *Psycho,* is there, as are the the the sets used in *Back to the Future* (the Hill Valley courthouse), *The Sting, McHale's Navy*, and the television series like "Murder She Wrote," "Matlock," "Leave It To Beaver," "The Munsters," and "Nancy Drew."

2. "BRADY BUNCH" HOUSE, 11222 Dilling Street
House used for the exterior of the popular television show, which aired from 1969 to 1974.

3. ACADEMY OF TELEVISION ARTS AND SCIENCES, 5220 Lankershim Boulevard (corner of Magnolia Boulevard)
Only the library is open to the general public, but outside the building itself is a Hall of Fame Plaza featuring bronze statutes of Lucille Ball, Jack Benny, Mary Tyler Moore, Johnny Carson and other members of the Academy's Hall of Fame.

4. CBS STUDIO CENTER, 4024 Radford Avenue
This studio has changed hands several times since Mack Sennett, "The King of Comedy," built it in 1928. It has variously been Mascot Pictures, Republic Studios, CBS Television Center, CBS/Fox Studios, and CBS/ MTM Studios. Many of the most memorable programs in television history have been produced here: "Rawhide," "Gunsmoke," "The Mary Tyler Moore

Show," "The Bob Newhart Show," "Rhoda," "Phyllis," "Lou Grant," "WKRP in Cincinnati," "Gilligan's Island," "The Wild, Wild West," "My Three Sons," "Hawaii Five-0," "Get Smart," "Hill St. Blues," "St. Elsewhere," "Remington Steele," "Falcon Crest," and "Roseanne." No tours; no visitors allowed.

5. LOS ANGELES VALLEY COLLEGE, 5800 Fulton Avenue

Danny DeVito took writing classes from Billy Crystal here in *Throw Momma From the Train.*

6. GRANT HIGH SCHOOL, 13000 Oxnard Street (at Coldwater Canyon)

Used for the filming of teen-oriented TV shows, including "The Wonder Years," "Life Goes On," and "Parker Lewis Can't Lose." "Beverly Hills 90210," which usually films at Torrance High School, has also used the high school for indoor classroom scenes. Alumni include Tom Selleck and Mitch Gaylord.

7. LITTLE BROWN CHURCH IN THE VALLEY, 4418 Coldwater Canyon

Ronald Reagan and Nancy Davis were married here on March 4, 1952.

CELEBRITIES WHO LIVE IN STUDIO CITY: Scott Baio, Adrienne Barbeau, Elayne Boosler, William Daniels and Bonnie Bartlett, Shelley Duvall, Erik Estrada, Helen Hunt, Erin Gray, Leonard Maltin, Michael McDonald, Roddy McDowell, Michael J. McKean, Alyssa Milano, Jay North, Ted Shackelford, William Shatner, Marc Singer, Patrick Swayze, Betty Thomas, Tina Turner, Joan Van Ark, Robb Weller, and George Wendt.

☆ SHERMAN OAKS, VAN NUYS AND ENCINO

1. MARILYN MONROE'S FIRST HONEYMOON HOME, 4524 Vista del Monte (one block west of Van Nuys Boulevard)

After marrying her first husband Jim Dougherty on June 19, 1942, an 18-year-old Norma Jean Baker (who later changed her name to Marilyn Monroe) lived in a one-room studio apartment here for a few months.

2. VAN NUYS HIGH SCHOOL, 6535 Cedros Avenue

One of the high schools used for the filming of "The Wonder Years" and "Life Goes On." *Fast Times at Ridgemont High* was also shot here. Famous alumni include Robert Redford, Don Drysdale, Natalie Wood, Paula Abdul, and Jane Russell. Marilyn Monroe attended school here for a year, but was not graduated.

3. SHERMAN OAKS GALLERIA, 15303 Ventura Boulevard

Moon Unit Zappa spoofed this once-notorious teen hangout—and the spoiled, cliquish teen-agers she met at Bar Mitzvah parties—in her hit song "Valley Girls." The Galleria was also site of the filming of *Fast Times at Ridgemont High, Commando,* and according to one mall official, "a lot of B movies we'd rather not talk about."

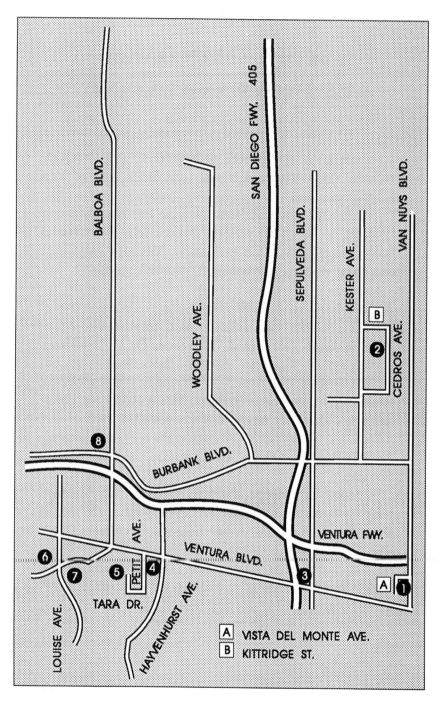

MAP 33 SHERMAN OAKS, VAN NUYS & ENCINO

4. FORMER HOME OF MICHAEL JACKSON, 4641 Hayvenhurst Avenue

The Gloved One moved his chimp Bubbles, giraffes, snakes, swans, and the rest of his zoo to a 2,700-acre ranch in the Santa Ynez Valley in Santa Barbara, but the this 8,000-square-foot home, where his parents reside, is still listed in his name.

5. "HOUSE OF TWO GABLES," 4543 Tara Drive

Gable lived here with three of his wives: Carole Lombard, Lady Sylvia Ashley and Kay Williams Spreckles. In 1977 the home was purchased by Michael R. Milken.

6. HOME OF KIRSTIE ALLEY AND PARKER STEVENSON, 4875 Louise Avenue

Alley lives in a mansion that Barbara Walters called "one of the loveliest homes I've ever seen." We do not know if she kept her promise, but according to Walters, Kirstie vowed to spend $400 a week on flowers in the home—the amount she used to spend for cocaine. Al Jolson originally built the house for Ruby Keeler. Alley also owns 300-acre ranch in Oregon and a 20-bedroom ocean-front home in Maine.

7. LONG-TIME HOME OF JOHN WAYNE, 4750 Louise Avenue

Wayne, a chain-smoker, lived here until he was stricken with lung cancer and decided to move to Newport Beach, where the air is easier to breathe.

8. BALBOA PARK, Balboa and Burbank Boulevards

The park is not exactly what you would call a tourist attraction—unless, of course, you go on

235

Saturdays to root for Michael Keaton, Tony Danza, Billy Crystal, and the other show business celebrities playing in the ShowBiz Softball League. Games are held on four diamonds every two hours between 9:00 A.M. and 5:00 P.M. NBC, Warner Bros., 20th Century Fox and other studios sponsor teams.

JUST OFF THE MAP in the northwest part of the San Fernando Valley, are a few sites that are historic for reasons other than entertainment. The 6.8-on-the-Richter-scale January 17, 1994 earthquake which devastated Los Angeles had its epicenter in the community of Northridge. 16 of the 57 deaths occurred when the top two floors of the Northridge Meadows Apartments at 9565 Reseda Blvd., collapsed on the bottom floor, killing tenants sleeping on the first level. (The earthquake also left an estimated 20,000 Angelinos homeless.)

Also off the map, in Lakeview Terrace, is the site of the March 3, 1991, Rodney King beating incident, which occurred on a dirt field across from the Mountainback Apartments at 11777 Foothill Boulevard. It was the most publicized incident of police brutality in the nation, and the April 28, 1992, acquittal of the four police officers who clubbed King 56 times led to the worst riots ever in the United States. (Two of the officers, Stacy Koon and Lawrence Powell, were subsequently convicted of federal charges.)

There are a few other movie and TV locations in the northern San Fernando Valley. The Ewing house featured on the hit TV series "Knots Landing" can be found on Crystalaire Place in Granada Hills. Also in Lakeview Terrace — at 11600 Eldridge Avenue in

Lakeview Terrace—is the former Lakeview Medical Center. The building would have been the Nancy Reagan Drug Center, but the residents of Lakeview Terrace, who objected to placing the center in their neighborhood, threatened to picket the Reagan Bel-Air mansion. Nancy withdrew her support for the project, and now the building is now used exclusively for motion picture and television filming. The most famous movie shot here is *Terminator II*. Lakeview served as Pescadero State Hospital, where a crazed Linda Hamilton was imprisoned and the two Terminators had one of their many confrontations. The hospital was also seen as the both hospitals in *Postcards from the Edge,* and was used for scenes in *Mr. Jones, Ricochet, Dying Young, Another 48 Hours, Heart Condition* and *Road House.*

CELEBRITIES WHO LIVE IN ENCINO AND SHERMAN OAKS: William Conrad, Robert Guillame, Tony Danza, Steve Kanaly, Albert Brooks, Shari Belafonte-Behrens, Gregory Harrison, Patrick Swayze, David Hasselhoff, Ana-Alicia, James Earl Jones, Michael Dorn, Gavin MacLeod, William Devane, David Leisure, Kristy McNichol, Barry Corbin, Rodney Dangerfield, Annette Funicello, LeVar Burton, Richard Crenna, David Nelson, Cybill Shepherd, Rue McClanahan, Steve Allen, Melissa Manchester, DeForest Kelley, Jean Smart and Richard Gilliland, Lesley Ann Warren, Ernie Banks, Darryl Strawberry, David Doyle, Robert Conrad, Dana Carvey, Smokey Robinson, Efrem Zimbalist, Jr., Graham Nash, Edward James Olmos, James Coburn, Ronnie Cox, Harlan Ellison, Judd Hirsch, Michael Reagan, Mike Farrell, Sara Gilbert, Hector Elizondo, Mel Harris and Cotter Smith, Mike Conners, Patty Duke, Lee Grant, Al Jarreau, Tom Petty, Tim and Daphne Reid, and Pat Sajak.

CELEBRITIES WHO LIVE IN VAN NUYS: Andy Garcia, James Earl Jones, Walter Koenig, and James Doohan. Nichele Nichols, James Brown, Greg Evigan, and Elgin Baylor live in Woodland Hills. Other San Fernando Valley residents include Jodie Foster, Patrick Duffy, Beau Bridges, Lisa Bonet, John Ashton, Bruce Boxleitner, Ted Lange, Nikki Sixx, John Davidson, Bob Eubanks, Jack Scalia, Howie Mandel, and Clayton Moore.

When Steven Spielberg's locations scouts searched for a house to use as Elliott's in *E.T.*, they looked for a typical suburban house that looked like it had a magical mountain and a redwood forest behind it. They found the house in the northwest section of the San Fernando Valley (7121 Lonzo Street, Tujunga), situated in front of one of the highest peaks of the San Gabriel Mountains. E.T. took up residence here after being stranded by his fellow travelers, and Elliott hid him until both were discovered by government agents. The Halloween street scenes and the chase scenes, though, were filmed on several different streets of Porter Ranch, another community in the northwestern portion of the San Fernando Valley. The famous scene in which Elliott and his friends, seemingly cornered by police cars, fly away into the air on their bicycles was filmed on White Oak Blvd. in Northridge, between Tribune and San Fernando Mission Roads.

☆ OTHER POINTS OF INTEREST IN OR NEAR LOS ANGELES

● **"NIGHTMARE ON ELM STREET" HOUSE,** 1428 N. Genessee Avenue, Hollywood

The two-story white house where Freddy Krueger ran amok is located in Hollywood, just south of Nichols Canyon.

● **HOUSE AT 1530 ORANGE GROVE AVENUE,** Hollywood

In *Halloween*, Jamie Lee Curtis lived at 1530 Orange Grove Avenue. A house across the street at 1533 was also filmed. The street, two blocks west of Genessee, is used frequently as a filming site because it does not have palm trees and looks midwestern.

● **SHOOTING OF MARVIN GAYE,** 2101 S. Gramercy Place

On February 18, 1985, the singer was shot to death by his father, Rev. Marvin Gaye, Sr., in Mid-City, a community south of Hancock Park.

● **"LEAVE IT TO BEAVER" HOME,** 1727 Buckingham Road

Not far from the Gaye shooting site is the home whose exterior was seen as the Cleaver family home in "Leave It to Beaver."

● **USC/COUNTY HOSPITAL,** 1200 N. State Street, East Los Angeles
Port Charles Hospital in "General Hospital."

● **GARFIELD HIGH SCHOOL,** 5101 E. Sixth Street, East Los Angeles
The movie *Stand and Deliver* was based on a true story about Garfield High School. The students, under-privileged and expected to underperform, were taught to excel in calculus for a state test by a teacher, Jaime Escalante, who was portrayed in the movie by Edward James Olmos. When the students performed well above average, the state testing agency accused the students of cheating and invalidated the scores. Given the choice of either accepting the testing service's decision or retest-ing, the stuents chose to "stand and deliver."

● **FORMER SITE OF LINCOLN FOUNDRY,** 2525 49th Street, Vernon
The police station and the motel room in the original *Terminator*. The plant was vacant at the time and has since been demolished.

● **SHAMROCK MEATS,** 3461 E. Vernon Avenue (corner Alcoa Avenue)
In the first *Rocky*, Sylvester Stallone worked here and practiced for prize fights by punching slabs of beef. Scenes from *The Mambo Kings* were also shot here.

● **KERN'S OF CALIFORNIA,** 13010 E. Temple Avenue, City of Industry
In the first *Terminator,* Arnold Schwarzenegger was crushed to death in this food manufacturing and canning facility.

● **CITADEL OUTLET SHOPPING MALL,** 5675 E. Telegraph Road, City of Commerce

Site of the fictional Delance Studios in the 1992 Yahoo Serious movie *Reckless Kelly*. The mall, which was once a Uniroyal tire factory, and which has been compared to an Assyrian palace, was also used for some of the scenes from the 1959 film *Ben-Hur*.

● **VENICE HIGH SCHOOL,** 13000 Venice Boulevard, Venice

One of the two high schools used as Rydell House School in *Grease*. There is a statue of Myrna Loy, a Warner Bros. star of the 1920s and a former Venice High School student, on the front lawn.

● **LOS ANGELES INTERNATIONAL AIRPORT**

The Washington airport scenes of *Die Hard II* were shot at LAX, and the producers forgot to conceal the LA-identifying "Pac Bell" notice on the pay phone used in a Bruce Willis scene. The Zucker-Abrahams-Zucker comedy *Airplane* is perhaps the most famous of the many movies filmed at LAX.

● **PORTOFINO INN,** 260 Portofino Way, Redondo Beach

In *Cannonball Run,* starring Burt Reynolds and dozens of other stars, the finish line of the cross-country speed car race was filmed extensively here.

● **KING HARBOR,** Beryl Street, Redondo Beach
Setting of TV's "Riptide."

● **TORRANCE HIGH SCHOOL,** 2200 West Carson Street, Torrance

The high school depicted as West Beverly High in "Beverly Hills 90210."

● **WAYFARER'S CHAPEL,** 5755 Palos Verdes Drive South, Rancho Palos Verdes

This unique glass-walled chapel, designed by Lloyd Wright, Frank Lloyd Wright's son, is a popular tourist attraction and is used frequently for movie wedding scenes, including Dennis Quaid and Meg Ryan's wedding in *Innerspace.* Jayne Mansfield, Dennis Hopper and "M*A*S*H" star Gary Burghoff were married here.

● **QUEEN MARY,** Pier J at end of Long Beach Freeway, Long Beach

The Queen Mary, one of the largest passenger liners ever built, has been in over 200 productions, most notably *The Poseidon Adventure. In Someone to Watch Over Me,* Mimi Rogers witnessed a murder in the swimming pool, which was transformed into a New York art museum (the producers put plexiglass over the pool).

● **PORT CAFE,** 955 S. Neptune Avenue, Wilmington (across from the Vincent Thomas Bridge)

In *When Harry Met Sally,* starring Meg Ryan and Billy Crystal, Ryan faked her orgasm here. The cafe shut down when part of Neptune closed and customers found it too difficult to find. The cafe is now used exclusively for filming.

● **MALIBU CREEK STATE PARK,** Las Virgenes Road (east of Las Virgenes Road/Malibu Canyon)

This park was once Century Ranch, a Twentieth Century Fox back lot. It was purchased by the State of California in 1974—and continues to be a frequent filming site. The park is probably best known as the site where incoming choppers brought in the wounded in television's "M*A*S*H" (as well as in the 1970 movie of the same name). The park has also been the site of the first and at least one *Planet of the Apes* sequel, of *Butch Cassidy and the Sundance Kid* (Robert Redford and Paul Newman jumped off a cliff here), and *Tora! Tora! Tora!*.

● **PARAMOUNT RANCH,** 1813 Cornell Road, Agoura (north of Malibu Creek State Park)

This national park was once owned by Paramount Studios. Still in existence here is a "Western Town," which includes a general store, wood shop, barn and bridge used in the filming of *The Virginian; Have Gun, Will Travel; The Riflemen; Bat Masterson* and dozens of other films and television series. Free tours are given on an irregular basis. Call (818) 597-9192 for additional information.

● **SIX FLAGS MAGIC MOUNTAIN,** 26101 Magic Mountain Parkway, off Interstate 5, (805) 255-4111

This large amusement park was Wally World in *National Lampoon's Vacation*. It has also doubled as Wisconsin Wonderland, the amusement park seen in the opening credits of the TV series "Step by Step," starring Patrick Duffy and Suzanne Somers.

244

● **VASQUEZ ROCKS COUNTY PARK,** 10700 Escondido Canyon Road, Agua Dulce (northeast of Newhall on Route 14)

Fodors calls it "one of Los Angeles County's best photo opportunities [even though] it's a two-hour drive from downtown." The main attractions are the unusual angular rocks that one might expect to encounter on an alien planet. Dozens of Western and science fiction movies (including *Star Trek* and *Star Wars)*, and television shows (the original "Star Trek") have been filmed there.

● **SANTA ANA TRAIN STATION,** 1000 E. Santa Ana Boulevard, Santa Ana

The place where Tom Cruise said goodbye to Dustin Hoffman in the final scene of *Rainman*; and where Chevy Chase, accompanied by Darryl Hannah, eluded his pursuers in *Memoirs of an Invisible Man.*

● **MAIN PLACE, SANTA ANA,** 2800 N. Main Street, Santa Ana

The mall where Arnold Schwarzenegger arrested Richard Tyson in *Kindergarten Cop.*

ACKNOWLEDGMENTS

There are so many people that I need to thank that it is difficult to know where to start. In researching this book, I interviewed or consulted with many location managers, operators of location services, publicists, librarians, real-estate agents, and other entertainment industry professionals.

Perhaps it would be fitting to start with the members of the various city and state film commissions: Dirk Beving and his staff at the City of Los Angeles Film and Video Permit Office; Lisa Mosher, librarian; Hugh Cooper, permit coordinator; and Amy Gutierrez, intern at the California Film Commission; Jason Hartman of the Los Angeles County Film Office; Ariel Penn, Film Liaison, city of Pasadena; Benita Miller, special event coordinator of Beverly Hills' Department of Public Services; Ian Tanza of the West Hollywood Film Commission; Christopher Reed, the former permit coordinator of Culver City; Richard Wiles, the battalion chief who issues permits for the city of Vernon; and Cheryl Adams of the Santa Clarita Film Commission.

I would like to especially thank Diane Klein, Antoinette Levine, Robin Citrin, Donald Potts, Jack English, Joseph Luizzi, Sr., and the other location managers, location scouts and operators of location services who helped me: Ned Shapiro, Steve Dawson, David Israel, Louis Goldstein, Paul Pav, Richard Davis, Bud Aronson, Annette Gahret, Peter Juliano, Billie

247

Jenkins, Marie Warren, Bruce Rush, Keith Kramer, Craig Pointes, Richard Rosenberg, Marvin Bernstein, Bob Craft, Amy Ness, Rhonda Baer, Taman McCall, David Preston, Ken Campbell, Mike Alvarado, Ken Rosen, Rick Rosen, Steph Benseman, Rowland Kirks, Ed Jeffers, Eva Schroeder, and Kris Wagner.

As well, Randy Young, past president of the Pacific Palisades Historical Society; Phyllis Lerner of the Beverly Hills Historical Society; Hope Keimon and Tonie Carnes of the Pasadena Historical Society; Betsy Goldman of the Venice Historical Society; Linda Brady of the Culver City Historical Society; Julie Lugocerra, Sony Pictures' liaison with the community and author of a forthcoming book on Culver City; Louise Gabriel of the Santa Monica Historical Society; and Dorothy Price and Sid Adair of the Windsor Square-Hancock Park Historical Society, were all very generous with their time and provided very helpful information.

Thanks also to the librarians who helped me research various topics, including Lisa Mosher of the California Film Commission; the staff of the Center for Motion Picture Studies in Beverly Hills; Shirley Kennedy and her staff at the Academy of Television Arts and Sciences; the librarians at the Los Angeles Public Library, Pasadena Public Library, and the Orange County Public Library, particularly the El Toro branch; Raymond Soto, UCLA Film and Television Librarian; Jennie Watts of the Huntington Library Rare Books Collection; Ken Kenyon of 20th Century Fox; Alline Merchant of the Brand Library; Tim Gregory of the Pasadena Historical Society; and Robert Tieman, assistant archivist, Walt Disney Studios.

Gary Sherwin, Director of Media Relations, and Connie Eldridge of the Los Angeles Convention and

248

Visitors Bureau, were most helpful; as were Jill Singer of the Donahue Group, which represents the Beverly Hills Visitors Bureau, and Victoria King of the Hotel Bel-Air. A number of other public relations professionals gave generously of their time, including Andy Marx; Lindsey Jones; Saul Kahan; Michael Klastorin; Paul Gendreau; Chris Tomasko; Denise Greenawalt; Doug Taylor; Liz Gengl; Richard Neely; John West; Fred Howard; Jill Tsukatoma; Rich Bornstein; Georgianna Francisco; Tom Gray; Teri Bond Michael, Karen Mack and Mary Tokita of UCLA; Tom Witherspoon of the Queen Mary; Diane Barnhardt of Cal Tech; Mary Blaze of Beverly Hills Hotel; Karen Wong of the Santa Monica Convention and Visitors Bureau; Harry Medved of the Screen Actors Guild; Kelly Greene of the Hollywood Roosevelt Hotel; Cliff Gallo of the American Film Institute; Kenlyn Elipsen of the Huntington; LuAnn Munns of Los Angeles State and County Arboretum; Barbara Leigh of the St. James Club; Maureen Stokes of The Biltmore (and David Morgan, who oversees filming there); Jim Yeager, director of publicity, Universal Studios Hollywood; Mike Rosenberg of the Los Angeles Coliseum; Julie Taylor of the Pacific Design Center; Rick Stevens of the California Highway Patrol; and Jeff Bliss of Pepperdine. And I certainly have not forgotten Marsha Meyer Sculatti of the West Hollywood Marketing Corporation; Luc Tamarra of the Los Angeles Unified School District; Kari Johnson, curator of the Hollywood Studio Museum; Al Davis, general manager of the Magic Castle; Mrs. Jay (Ramona) Ward of Dudley Doo-Rite Emporium; Nicky Blair; Denise Carrejo of Damar; Dee Stanley, Walker Location Services; Kevin Beggs of the "Baywatch" production staff; Judith Price, banquet manager, Columbia Bar and Grill; Doug MacArthur, manager of the Yamashiro; Judy Hunter, executive director of the Pasadena Historical Society; Don Zepfel, vice president, production, Universal Studios; Beth Savage, executive assistant of Raleigh Studios; Lorraine Shaw, Hollywood Center Studios, business affairs; Debbie Ross, manager of the Montecito Apartments; Ana Martinez-Holler of the Hollywood Walk of Fame; Manny Weltman, whose passion for historical accuracy should be shared by more chroniclers of Hollywood history; Stephanie Pond-Smith of Carolco; Eileen Garcia, president of the South Pasadena Chamber of Commerce; Steve Rose, president of the Culver City Chamber of Commerce; Dee Powers, owner of the Port Cafe; Josh Avin, manager of the Mondrian; Randall Makinson, director and curator of the Gamble House; Timothy Buchanan, principal of Burroughs High School; Don Waldrop, president, Franklin Hills Residents Association; Raoul H. Pinno, Film and Photo Shoot Manager, UCLA; Patricia Cohen Samuels of Spago; Richard Terra, vice president, Shamrock Meats; Nelson Crispo, USC Film Coordinator; Steve Harris, manager of the Castle Green Apartments, Pasadena; Norma Tomkinson of the J. W. Marriott Hotel; Tom O'Brien, personnel director, Kern's of California; John Schumacher, owner, and Clarence H. Brown, former owner of C. C. Brown; Jane Gilman, editor of the *Larchmont Chronicle*; Rick Rossini, assistant principal Van Nuys High School; Tom Buckley, film coordinator of Union Station; Gabriel Ramirez, manager of Cal Tech's Athenaeum; Susan Thompson of the Westin Bonaventure; Ruth Richards of the South Pasadena Preservation Society; Andy Stamatin of the Shrine Auditorium; Robin Faulk, marketing director, Santa Monica Place; Joe Walker, assistant principal, Grant High School; Bob Sirchia, vice president of Culver Studios; Ellen West and Ed Giles of the Department of Water and Power; Mark Stokhaug, Director of Security for 444 S. Flower Street; Richard Adkins, executive director, Hollywood Studio Museum; Ruth Ryon and Steve Harvey of the *Los Angeles Times;* Richard Taylor, head security, fire and security, Warner Hollywood Studios; Tracy Fowler of the Century Plaza Hotel and Towers; Barbara Rosenman of Los Angeles Parks and Recreation (Greystone); Joseph DiSante, manager of guest services, ABC TV; Stephanie DeWolf, assistant planner, and Randy Shulman, planning intern, of the Pasadena Urban Conservation Department; Officer Chuck Foote, Los Angeles Police Academy; Sgt. Larry Thompson, Los Angeles Police Department film coordinator; Richard Munitz, assistant principal, Beverly Hills High School; Marge Maple of Hollywood Memorial Park Cemetery; Karen Sanders of the Pasadena Convention and Visitors Bureau; Norma LeValley, editor, *South Pasadena Review;* Charlie Morton, owner "Dynasty" house; Peter Pampush, assistant director, student affairs, USC School of Cinema and Television; Bob Bacon of Ramsey-Shilling Realtors; Deborah Bieber and Denise Mathis of Bellefontaine School; Sandra Griffin, property manager of the El Royale Apartments; David Bowen of "Step by Step;" Jodi Hutchinson of Six Flags Magic Mountain; Judy Bijlani, marketing director, Main Place, Santa Ana; Cecyle Rexrode and Shirley Krims of Warner Bros.; Connie Humburger of LA Conservancy; Carolyn Lucci of the Sherman Oaks Galleria; Paul Garcia, buildings and grounds manager of the Wayfarers Chapel; Ellen Appel Public Relations; Larry Paull; Emily Ferry; Marcia Reed and Jim Bissel.

Jeff Hutner, author of *The LA Bargain Book,* and his assistant Linda Roberts; Kathryn Leigh Scott of Pomegranate Press; Julie von Zerneck and Joseph Naud of Portrait of a Bookstore; Steven Abrams; and Paul Keane, all provided valuable advice which I appreciate.

And finally, I'd like to thank those involved in the production of this book, including my editor, Lisa Rojany, for her invaluable and painstaking editorial expertise; my designer, Richard Adkins; and Julian Wasser, who provided many of the photographs included here. My apologies to anyone I inadvertently left out.

A NOTE ABOUT FUTURE EDITIONS

The Ultimate Hollywood Tour Book will be updated regularly, and future editions will include the filming locations of motion pictures released after mid-1992, as well as updated listings and additional points of interest. If you know of a filming location not mentioned in this book—and if we use the information, subject, of course, to verification—we will send you a free copy of the second edition of the book. Tips should be sent to:

North Ridge Books
P.O. Box 2314
Toluca Lake, CA 91610

ABOUT THE AUTHOR

William A. Gordon is a freelance writer and the author of two previous books, *The Fourth of May: Killings and Coverups at Kent State* and *"How Many Books Do You Sell in Ohio?:" A Quote Book for Writers*. The Kent State book, published in 1990, was praised as the definitive book on the killings by the *Detroit Free Press. Choice* magazine called it "as entertaining as the best detective fiction and as analytical and as well documented as the best journalism or scholarship."

The quotation book, published in 1986, was selected by the Writer's Digest Book Club and was well-received despite its title (one of the quotations in the book and a commentary on the state of book publishing today). Cleveland's *Plain Dealer* called it "very enjoyable;" the *Evening Post* of Charleston, S.C., called it "a delight to read;" and *Wilson Library Bulletin* called it "irresistible . . . Gordon has succeeded in selecting the most memorable, thought-provoking, important, funny and/or outrageous quotations about the book world." Mr. Gordon is a former resident of Akron, Ohio, and currently lives in Los Angeles.

INDEX

Moss, Jerome, 46
Mr. Baseball, 106, 206
"Mr. Novak," 195
Mr. Saturday Night, 174
MRX Pharmacy, 173
Mulholland Estates, 179
Mulholland House, 183
Mulligan, Richard, 56
Murphy, Eddie, 144, 213
Musso and Frank Grill, 152
Mutual Benefit Life, 168

Naked Gun, The, 175
National Enquirer, 125
NBC, 223, 224
Nelson, Ozzie and Harriet, 143, 211
Nelson, Rick, 143, 183
Newhart, Bob, 46
Newsies, 209, 210
Nicholson, Jack, 143, 179, 180
Nightmare on Elm Street, 240
9 to 5, 48
Nixon, Richard M., 69
North, Jay, 212
Northridge Mall, 98

Ocean Front Walk, 94
O'Connor, Carroll, 65
Olive, The, 167
Olmos, Edward James, 241
Opportunity Knocks, 174
Orion Pictures, 110
O'Rourke, Heather, 107
Other People's Money, 172
Ovitz, Michael, 70, 88, 107, 112
Owlwood, 56
Oziel, Jerome, 63
Pacific Design Center, 134
Pacific Heights, 110
Pacific Palisades High School, 76
Pantages Theater, 156
Paradise Cove, 85
Paramount Studios, 161, 162
Parker Center, 203

Parker, Dorothy, 133
"Partridge Family, The," 226
Pasadena City Hall, 212
Pasadena Police Station (Former), 210
Pasadena Public Library, 211
Pashdag, John, 34, 48
Patrick's Roadhouse, 100
Paty's Restaurant, 226
Peck, Gregory, 41
Penn, Sean, 87
Pepperdine University, 84
Perfect, 133
Perrenchio, Jerrold, 44
Phillips, John, 42, 44
Phillips, Michelle, 42, 44
Phillips, Lou Diamond, 226
Pickfair, 29
Pickford, Mary, 29, 159, 173
Planet of the Apes, 88, 245
Playboy Mansion, 54, 55
Playboy Studio West, 124
Player, The, 121, 158, 168, 210, 216
Plaza del Sol, 123
Plunkett, Hugh, 21
Point Dume, 87
Poitier, Sidney, 25
Polanski, Roman, 32, 179
Portrait of a Bookstore, 226
Poseidon Adventure, The, 243
Postcards From the Edge, 84, 238
Powell, Dick, 70
Presley, Elvis, 19, 40, 96
Presley, Priscilla, 19, 40
Pretty in Pink, 200
Pretty Woman, 66, 121, 152, 200
Prince, 20, 63
Prince, Hal, 63
"Pros and Cons," 121
Pryor, Richard, 236
Psycho, 229, 230
Quaid, Dennis, 84
"Queen For a Day," 156

PHOTO CREDITS

All photographs are © 1992 William A. Gordon except as indicated. Page 23 (Beverly Hills Hotel), 33 (Manson Murder Site), 45 (Ronald Reagan/"Beverly Hillbillies" houses), 50 (Spelling mansion), and 55 (Playboy Mansion), © 1992 Julian Wasser. Page 65 (Regent Beverly Wilshire) courtesy Beverly Hills Visitors Bureau/© Martin Elkort. Pages 68, 69 and 75 (Roseanne Arnold, Marilyn Monroe and Arnold Schwarzenegger homes) © 1992 Julian Wasser. Page 78 (Thelma Todd Café) courtesy Randy Young/Pacific Palisades Historical Society. Page 83 (Malibu Colony), 86 (Unger/Carson estates) and 90 (Broad Beach) © 1992 Julian Wasser. Page 97 (Santa Monica Pier) courtesy Santa Monica Convention and Visitors Bureau/Justine Hill. Page 109 (Century City) and 118 (Chateau Marmont) © 1992 Julian Wasser. Page 120 (St. James Club) courtesty West Hollywood Marketing Corporation/Jim McHugh; 135 (Tail o' the Pup) courtesy West Hollywood Marketing Corporation. Page 145 (Mann's Chinese Theater) courtesy Cinamerica Theaters. Page 146 (Hollywood Walk of Fame), and 154 (Capitol Records) courtesy Los Angeles Convention and Visitors Bureau/© 1991 Michele and Tom Grimm. Page 180 (Jack Nicholson home) © 1992 Julian Wasser. Page 192 (Griffith Park Observatory), and 202 (City Hall), courtesy Los Angeles Convention and Visitors Bureau/© 1991 Michele and Tom Grimm. Page 205 Shrine Auditorium, courtesy Shrine Auditorium & Exposition Center. Page 211 (Gamble House) courtesy Pasadena Convention and Visitors Bureau. Page 218 (Queen Anne cottage) courtesy Los Angeles State and County Arboretum. Page 225 (Warner Bros.) © 1992 Julian Wasser. Page 229 (Universal Studios) © 1990 Universal City Studios.

THE HOLLYWOOD BOOKSHELF

Books of related interest that can be ordered from North Ridge Books:

❏ **Hollywood at Your Feet: The Story of the World-Famous Chinese Theater** by Stacey Endres and Bob Cushman.
With over 350 photographs. $19.95 (California residents add $1.65 sales tax).

❏ **Hollywood Goes On Location: A Guide to Famous Movie and TV Sites** by Leon Smith.
Walk in the footsteps of screen legends—Bogart's Casablanca, Nicholson's *Chinatown*, Swanson's *Sunset Boulevard*, Superman's Daily Planet—all in the Los Angeles area. $16.95 (California residents add $1.40 sales tax).

❏ **Following the Comedy Trail: A Guide to Laurel and Hardy and Our Gang Film Locations** by Leon Smith.
Includes exact addresses and maps. $16.95 (California residents add $1.40 sales tax).

❏ **Lobby Cards: The Classic Films and Lobby Cards: The Classic Comedies,** both by Kathryn Leigh Scott.
Rare and magnificently designed full-color lobby cards; the first from classic motion pictures; the second from classic comedies. $35.00 each (California residents add $2.89 sales tax per book).

❏ **Word of Mouth: A Guide to Commercial Voice-Over Excellence** by Susan Blu and Molly Ann Mullin.

Book and cassette. Want to do voice-overs for local radio stations or commercials? The book is packed with techniques and tips and includes a special section on animation. The 50-minute cassette includes exercises, sample copy, professional demos and audition material. $19.95 (California residents add $1.65 sales tax).

❏ **The L.A. Bargain Book** by Jeff Hutner

Tips on how to save money; for both L.A. residents and those vacationing here. The best deals for accommodations, food, entertainment and shopping. $12.95 (California residents add $1.07 sales tax).

OTHER BOOKS BY WILLIAM A. GORDON

❏ **The Fourth of May: Killings and Coverups at Kent State**

This investigation of "the most popular murders ever committed in the United States" argues that the Ohio National Guardsmen were ordered to fire at students protesting the Vietnam War. $23.95 (California residents add $1.98 sales tax.)

Please send me the following books:

❑ Hollywood at Your Feet: The Story of the
   World-Famous Chinese Theater $19.95
❑ Hollywood Goes On Location $16.95
❑ Following the Comedy Trail $16.95
❑ Lobby Cards: The Classic Films $35.00
❑ Lobby Cards: The Classic Comedies $35.00
❑ Word of Mouth: Book and Cassette $19.95
❑ The L.A. Bargain Book $12.95
❑ The Fourth of May $23.95

Check the books you would like and add $3.00 shipping and handling for the first book; and an additional $1.00 for each additional book. The maximum shipping and handling cost is $7.50.

California residents must add 8.25% sales tax. Add $1.65 for Hollywood at Your Feet; $1.40 for Hollywood Goes on Location; $1.40 for Following the Comedy Trail; $2.89 for Lobby Cards: The Classic Films; $2.89 for Lobby Cards: The Classic Comedies; $1.65 for Word of Mouth; $1.07 for L.A. Bargain Book; and $1.98 for Fourth of May.

    (Please check your math very carefully. Incorrect amounts cannot be fulfilled.) Allow 4-6 weeks delivery.

Send check or money order payable to:
NORTH RIDGE BOOKS
P.O. Box 2314, Toluca Lake, CA 91610-0314
Cash or CODs will not be accepted.
Ship book to:
Mr./Mrs./Ms. _____
Address _____
City/State/Zip _____

Additional copies of

THE ULTIMATE
HOLLYWOOD
TOUR BOOK

can also be ordered by sending $15.95 and
$3.00 shipping and handling to:

NORTH RIDGE BOOKS
P.O. BOX 2314
TOLUCA LAKE, CA 91610

California residents please add $1.31 sales tax.